Alexis de Tocqueville

Twayne's World Authors Series

French Literature

David O'Connell, Editor
Georgia State University

TWAS 848

ALEXIS DE TOCQUEVILLE, BY LÉON NOËL

The Beinecke Rare Book and Manuscript Library, Yale University

Alexis de Tocqueville

Matthew Mancini

Southwest Missouri State University

Twayne Publishers • New York
Maxwell Macmillan Canada • Toronto
Maxwell Macmillan International • New York Oxford Singapore Sydney

Alexis de Tocqueville
Matthew Mancini

Twayne Publishers   Maxwell Macmillan Canada, Inc.
Macmillan Publishing Company   1200 Eglinton Avenue East
866 Third Avenue   Suite 200
New York, New York 10022   Don Mills, Ontario M3C 3N1

Library of Congress Cataloging-in-Publication Data

Mancini, Matthew.
    Alexis de Tocqueville / Matthew Mancini.
        p.   cm.—(Twayne's world authors series ; TWAS 848. French literature)
    Includes bibliographical references and index.
    ISBN 0-8057-4305-7
    1. Tocqueville, Alexis de, 1805–1859. 2. Tocqueville, Alexis de, 1805–1859—
Political and social views. 3. Historians—France—Biography. I. Title. II. Series:
Twayne's world authors series. French literature.
DC36.98.T63M36   1994   93-36335
944'.007202—dc20   CIP

10 9 8 7 6 5 4 3 2 1

Printed in the United States of America

To my mother, Catherine Mancini, and the memory of my father,
Joseph E. Mancini (1909–1988)

Contents

Preface

Tocqueville has been fortunate in his commentators. At every stage since George Wilson Pierson's 1938 classic, *Tocqueville and Beaumont in America*, numerous outstanding intellectuals on both sides of the Atlantic have devoted their energies to interpreting and explaining his life and work. Nowhere is this more evident than in the American academy. Pierson was followed by scholars of the stature of Seymour Drescher and Richard Herr, and now a new generation that includes such authorities as Roger Boesche and James T. Schleifer is reinterpreting Tocqueville for a postmodern and perhaps postliberal world.

Yet for all the critical richness of the work on Tocqueville, there remain lacunae in both interpretation and simple explanation. Rereading *Democracy in America* some years ago, for instance, I was struck by the force with which Tocqueville makes distinctions between ideas and feelings. The existence of this distinction in Tocqueville has long been recognized, to be sure, but it seemed to me to be central to his understanding of what was happening to the innermost souls of people in a democracy. Moreover, with a full understanding of this division or separation, I realized, we also approach the very heart of his understanding of the phenomenon of modernity. Similarly, I have been struck by Tocqueville's confrontation with nature and what his century called "the sublime." Or, again, by the relation between the formal theories of race that were emerging in the mid-nineteenth century and Tocqueville's fears about political apathy. There is so much yet to be said about Tocqueville: certainly this is one sign, at least, of a great thinker.

Then, too, for all the excellence of Tocqueville scholarship, a need still exists for a comprehensive, yet brief, study. No such attempt has been made since Hugh Brogan's volume in the Modern Masters series appeared in 1973. That book, with fewer than 90 pages, is really an extended essay. Acute in its critical intelligence, it is, however, far from comprehensive. Other outstanding recent studies, such as those by Roger Boesche, Doris Goldstein, Alan Kahan, and L. E. Shiner, are devoted to a particular theme or work of Tocqueville's.

This book has two main objectives. First, it situates Tocqueville's works in the context of the turbulent world in which he lived and wrote.

Second, it seeks to demonstrate why Tocqueville has been placed in the small circle of political and social thinkers considered indispensable to an understanding of our modern condition. In this book, I consider all of Tocqueville's major and many of his minor works, always in light of the political, economic, social, and intellectual context that produced them. My goal is to help readers, whether they be experts or neophytes, understand Tocqueville's relevance for us as inheritors of the world he did so much to explain, even as it was being shaped.

I begin with a biographical chapter, the theme of which is Tocqueville's attempt to come to terms with a completely new (as it seemed) kind of world, one we have since learned to call modern. In it I try to clarify both Tocqueville and modernity by stressing their reciprocal interaction. Chapters 2 and 3 comprise a detailed exegesis of Tocqueville's greatest work, *Democracy in America*, which was published in 1835 and 1840 and established his reputation. In chapter 4, I examine Tocqueville's understanding of certain of society's "outsider" groups, such as paupers, prisoners, and Native Americans. Some of his most fascinating writings can be found in his investigations of such urgent social questions as crime and poverty. What is more, they seem to be of a piece with his more famous political works on democracy and revolution, revealing a constant preoccupation with the promises and perils of democratic equality, despotism, and political apathy. Chapter 5 contains an analysis of Tocqueville's writings on slavery, a subject on which he was one of the leading authorities of his era. Accompanying the discussion on slavery are related analyses of the larger question of race and of French imperialism in Africa. The examination reveals ruinous moral and intellectual inconsistencies in Tocqueville's thought. A pioneer French abolitionist, a humane observer of the industrial and urban poverty of his own time, he also defended the subjugation of Algeria as France's highest duty to herself. Part of chapter 5 is a revised version of an essay that appeared in *Slavery and Abolition* 10 (September 1989): 151–71; and I thank that journal for allowing me to make use of that material in this new context. In the sixth and final chapter, I try to elucidate Tocqueville's analysis of revolution, that dangerous viral strain of the promising new democratic era.

I too have been fortunate in my commentators. Over the past few years, as this book was taking shape, colleagues and friends from several institutions have given me invaluable help, criticism, and encouragement. To name all of them would add a chapter to this book; but, on the other hand, the kindnesses rendered by a few stand out from the rest and fairness permits them to be singled out. Tulane University's Murphy Institute of Political Economy generously granted me a Faculty Research Fellowship, as a result of which I was able not only to complete a portion of this study, but also to harvest the benefits of astute criticism in an environment that promotes a high level of intellectual striving and achievement. Grateful acknowledgment is also due to the National Endowment for the Humanities, which sponsored two summer seminars that provided opportunities for extended research and writing—again in the presence of intellectually demanding and stimulating colleagues. At Tulane, Richard Teichgraeber III, Marilyn Brown, and Bill McClay, and at Rice University, Thomas Haskell and Alan Kahan, gave invaluable readings of large portions of the manuscript. Stanley Engerman, of the University of Rochester, a distinguished scholar in a field seemingly far removed from Tocqueville studies, has an unshakable commitment to the best scholarship in any field; his criticisms of my treatment of Tocqueville's economic thought were essential. Also very helpful were Fordham University's Merold Westphal and Deal Hudson, who have read almost every line I have written in the last ten years; and Southwest Missouri State University's Dominic J. Capeci, Jr. and Bernice Warren, the former a discerning and erudite student of the history of American race relations, and the latter a ruthless comma-cutter as well as a dean who supports research by all available means. Closer to home, Philip asked only relevant questions, while Nancy criticized and supported in measures that were exactly correct for their recipient.

Chronology

Chapter One

Neither a Pleasure Nor a Sorrow: The Life of a Voyager

A Young Aristocrat under the Restoration

Louise-Madeline Le Peletier de Rosanbo, Comtesse de Tocqueville, bore three sons: Hippolyte, Edouard, and, in Paris on 29 July 1805, Alexis. The boys were destined to grow up in a strange and turbulent world, for the larger-than-life figures and events of the French Revolution loomed over the family history of the Tocquevilles as it did over their nation. During the Terror of 1793, only weeks after their wedding, Louise and her new husband, Hervé Clérel de Tocqueville, were locked away in the prison of Port-Royal. Louise's father, then her grandfather, the celebrated Lamoignon de Malesherbes, who had come out of retirement to defend Louis XVI before the Convention, were guillotined. Her older sister and her brother-in-law, who was the brother of the great romantic writer René-François de Chateaubriand, were executed as well. Louise and Hervé were spared only by Robespierre's fall. Their two orphaned Chateaubriand nephews would be raised in the same household with Hippolyte, Edouard, and Alexis.

During the years of Napoleon's ascendancy over France and Europe, the Comte de Tocqueville lived quietly with his family at the château of the little village of Verneuil in Normandy (where he was mayor) during the summers, and in Paris in winter. But in 1814, with the defeat of Napoleon and the ensuing restoration of the Bourbon dynasty, the family fortunes took a different turn. In the next few years Hervé was appointed prefect, or departmental administrator, in various departmental capitals—Angers, Beaurais, Dijon, Metz.

In 1820, Alexis, then living in Paris with the rest of his family, was summoned by his lonesome father to join him at Metz. He enrolled in the Metz *lycée*, where he performed with great distinction, winning among other awards the first prize in rhetoric. It was in this provincial city on the Moselle in Lorraine, about 180 miles due east of Paris, that an episode occurred that has assumed a sort of legendary stature among close students of Tocqueville—and a few who are not so close, as well. Left to his own devices in a grand and largely empty château, the precocious and sensitive youngster took to spending long hours in his father's library. There, at the age of 16, he delved into the works of the skeptical *lumières* of the eighteenth century and suffered a loss of religious conviction, the emotional and intellectual effects of which were devastating and permanent. "Until that time, my life had passed enveloped in a faith that had not allowed doubt to penetrate into my soul," he recalled 35 years later. "Then doubt entered . . . not only doubt about one thing or another in particular, but an all-embracing doubt. . . . I was seized by the blackest melancholy . . . and was almost prostrated by agitation and terror at the sight of the road that remained for me to travel in this world."[1]

The sudden rush of doubt proved to be a formative experience for Tocqueville, whose early education had been in the hands of an aging, intelligent, kind, and devoted priest, Abbé Lesueur. "Bébé," as the boys affectionately called him, had been Hervé's tutor as well. Through him, Alexis had learned to associate religion with comfort and compassion. When these warm sentiments were chilled by the icy winds of reason, Tocqueville learned something that would decisively shape his world view. Henceforth, the introduction of this breach between feeling and idea, emotion and thought, would stand for him formally as a paradigm of the essential dilemma of the modern world, and subjectively as the moment of his personal loss of innocence. As he would write years later in the first part of *Democracy in America*, referring explicitly to the struggle between religion and democracy that he felt France had been tragically destined to endure, "That harmony which has been observed throughout history between the feelings and the ideas of men seems to have been destroyed."[2] Thus did he experience the "disenchantment of the world" that Max Weber would identify as a defining characteristic of modernity. Tocqueville's youthful encounter in the Metz library induced a dissonance between head and heart that he would later put forward as a distinguishing characteristic of our wounded, modern human condition.

Yet, an important point needs to be emphasized here because there has been a tendency to misconstrue this intriguing episode. Its result was to make Tocqueville a nonbeliever, not an unbeliever—that is, someone who was deprived of the comforting certainty of religious faith, not someone who actively disbelieved. The tenets of his childhood faith might, he thought, very well be true, but he could not be certain. In short, he *doubted*. All his life he loved in his heart the Church's sweet and salutary doctrines—the indisputable existence of a loving God, the immortality of the soul—as well as its moving liturgy. But his intellect would not permit these beliefs and practices to induce emotional security. In America, in the fall of 1831, Tocqueville suddenly interrupted the flow of the thoughts he was scribbling in his notebook—thoughts about, of all things, the effects of election on the powers of New England town officials—to list "doubt" as, along with death and sickness, one of the three chief miseries of mankind.[3]

In Metz, Tocqueville experienced only an inchoate depression and fear. The full consequences of this rupture between thought and feeling for his analysis of democracy would become evident only in the future. Being 16, however, he did manage to lift himself out of despondency, largely, as he recounted to his trusted friend Madame Swetchine, due to the effects of "violent passions," which reconnected him to the world of the senses and brought his mind back to earth.[4] He fell deeply in love with a spirited and charming *bourgeoise*, Rosalie Malye. Their relationship was not destined to end in marriage, however; their class differences led to their being separated after an affair of some five years' duration. Although this rift brought great pain to both, Tocqueville soon made the acquaintance of another captivating woman, Mary Mottley, whom he would eventually marry. Miss Mottley was if anything even more "unsuitable" than Mlle Malye. Not only was she nine years older than Alexis, bourgeois, and lacking a fortune, but she was English as well!

Long before his marriage, however, Tocqueville's education had proceeded apace. After he finished the course of study at the lycée, Alexis returned to Paris, where he studied law for three years, from 1823 to 1826. Neither the system of law studies nor Alexis's performance seems to have been particularly distinguished. According to André Jardin, thanks to whom there is now, finally, a definitive biography, "it is hard to discern the future author of the *Democracy*" in Tocqueville's unimpressive law thesis.[5] However, he was able to obtain an appointment (actually the position was created for him as a favor to his father) as juge auditeur, a kind of apprentice judge, in the Versailles courts. From 1827 to the revolutionary year of 1830, the young Tocqueville patiently observed the nuts and bolts of French civil law—and began to develop a hunger for fame and achievement that he could neither lose nor fully satisfy for the rest of his life.

At some time between finishing law studies and taking up his duties in Versailles, Alexis took the first of his many voyages. He and his broth-

er Edouard embarked on what was then a traditional excursion for aristocratic young men who had completed their formal studies: a tour of
Italy. The brothers' journey, however, was somewhat out of the ordinary,
as they left the main path of the grand tour for an expedition to Sicily.

This experience, too, made a deep impression on Alexis. He wrote a
long meditation on the adventure of some 350 pages, most of which has
since been lost. In the remaining fragments, he expresses for the first time
in his extant writings a fear of exile that is another indication of his sense
of precariousness and instability. An aristocrat in democratic times, is the
cliché by which the tension in Tocqueville is often expressed. But the
Metz incident, combined with a deep, almost painful affection for France
evident in the fragments from Sicily, are tokens of a much more complex
sense of the volatility of the times that were thrust upon him.[6]

In France itself, that volatility could not be contained, and the elements in the unstable mixture of French society, politics, and ideas
exploded in the Revolution of July 1830. Tocqueville was at that time
living in Versailles and, as juge auditeur, working diligently at his career.
The revolution would be a true turning point in his life. The social history of the July Revolution is complex and tragic, but its political results
are simply summarized. The increasingly despotic Bourbon monarch,
Charles X, was deposed, and with him the dynasty he and a century of
his forebears had done so much to discredit. The Bourbons, however,
were not replaced by a republic, as so many had hoped, but by a member of a collateral line, the Duke of Orleans, who came to the throne as
Louis Philippe. The July Monarchy that was thus established would last
until the Revolution of February 1848.

The last king of the French (as Louis Philippe was styled) was portrayed with biting satire by Tocqueville many years later in his
Recollections. But at the time of his ascension, he showed energy, persistence, and tact. Nevertheless, many members of the aristocracy could
not stomach him or his line, and retreated into a kind of internal exile,
having nothing to do with the state or its business. Many of those aristocrats, like Hervé de Tocqueville, had faithfully served the Bourbons in
important administrative positions. Now they withdrew. Among those
who chose quietude and noninvolvement were most of Alexis's family
and several of his friends, including his cousin and closest confidant,
Louis de Kergorlay.

Thus, when all government employees were required to take an oath
of loyalty to the new regime, Alexis was faced with a critical decision.
Knowing that his family would not agree, however, he decided to acqui-

esce and took the oath on 16 August. His inner turmoil was real enough. He wrote to Mary Mottley of his painful feeling of inner division: "I am at war with myself."[7] But the anguish was not due to a crisis of conscience. It came because, in thus declaring his allegiance, he was in a limited but real sense imposing a sentence of self-exile. The social upheaval represented by the crisis and revolution of July 1830, he had already come to feel, was the manifestation of inescapable new social forces only dimly understood even by the participants in the revolution. These were the new energies of equality and liberty that were destined to displace the values of the aristocratic milieu that had nurtured Tocqueville, his family, and almost all his friends (except, significantly, his women friends).

One crucial male friend, however, also took the requisite oath: Gustave de Beaumont, a deputy public prosecutor in Paris, who had held the same office in Versailles when Tocqueville first took up his duties there and with whom Tocqueville had shared quarters. From the first, these two young men shared a strong attachment and affinity for each other. Early on, Tocqueville wrote Beaumont of "a friendship that, I do not know how, was born *already full-grown* between us."[8] Beaumont's was without doubt the crucial friendship of Tocqueville's life. No passage in Tocqueville's enormous correspondence is as moving, perhaps, as that in the second-to-last letter he wrote, knowing he was dying, written from Cannes to Gustave in Paris, with its echoing plea to restore him to the field of action: "VENEZ. VENEZ. *Vous seul* pouvez nous remettre en campagne. . . . Venez. . . . Venez" ("COME. COME. *You alone* can return us to the field. . . . Come. . . . Come").[9]

Beaumont, too, was both uncomfortable under the new regime and convinced of its inevitability and its potential for orderly freedom. Gradually, the two friends formed a bold resolution. They would leave France for the United States to study the customs, laws, and institutions of the new kind of society whose dim outlines they could perceive through the smoke and dust of the July Revolution.

The distinguished French historian François Furet has argued that Tocqueville's decision to study the United States was made in solitude as much as five years before he and Beaumont actually left.[10] And it is entirely credible, although based on only one sliver of documentary evidence, to contend that the 20-year-old Tocqueville, whose parents' experiences formed the subject matter of his life's work, would have seen the United States as an uncontaminated example of the democratic future that in France was so mixed with other elements. But surely, too, the

1830 revolution, conversations with Beaumont, and both men's discomfort with the new dynasty, acted as catalysts, crystallizing what had been a much vaguer urge, something perhaps closer to a hope than a resolution, into a concrete plan.

Once made, however, the decision was pursued with ardor. Tocqueville and Beaumont received the 1830s equivalent of a government grant: they procured from the new government of Louis Philippe papers authorizing them on the government's behalf to visit the United States in order to study and report on its prison system. Over the years, the United States had attracted a stream of inquisitive foreign travelers who reported to an avid reading public on the odd manners and institutions the Americans had developed. Books by such visitors constituted a minor literary industry. Few institutions had aroused the interest of earnest Europeans more than the Americans' unique invention, the penitentiary. Although it is in some measure true that the investigation of the prisons was, as Tocqueville wrote to his good friend Eugène Stoffels, a mere "excuse" for their journey,[11] at the same time it should be noted that Tocqueville and Beaumont, a juge auditeur and a prosecuting attorney, were seriously interested in the subject, and gave their official duties a high priority throughout their journey. Moreover, the work they produced in consequence, *On the Penitentiary System in the United States*, is still considered an outstanding description and analysis of pre–Civil War American prisons.

On 2 April 1831, at Le Havre, the two friends embarked on the most important journey of their lives. Their visit to America occupied the nine months from 11 May 1831 to 20 February 1832. What they saw—both society and nature—astonished them.

Tocqueville and the Sublime: "Journey to Lake Oneida" and "A Fortnight in the Wilds"

Tocqueville, in particular, was taken aback by the American wilderness. In his notebooks and essays from the journey, we may see how he assimilated his encounters with wild nature into the theoretical structure that his time and place had at its disposal for understanding such experiences. That doctrine was known as the theory of the sublime. Its classic formulation occurred in a youthful work by the great conservative philosopher, Edmund Burke (1729–97).

In recent years, scholars from different viewpoints have given us a new perspective on Burke's theory of the sublime. In particular, these scholars have marshaled a significant body of evidence to show that Burke's career considered as a whole has an unexpected coherence to it. The ideas of the young Irishman who penned his *Philosophical Enquiry into . . . the Sublime and Beautiful* while still in his twenties are directly connected with the dread forewarnings of the Jeremiah of the House of Commons thundering about the diabolic French Revolution. Many links exist between the aesthetic categories of the sublime and the beautiful, on the one hand, and the political categories of power and submission, on the other.[12]

Meanwhile, although Tocqueville studies are livelier than ever, few scholars have examined the strong notes of the sublime in his own youthful works.[13] Yet such echoes are clearly evident, and Tocqueville himself left behind copious testimony to their importance in his emotional life. In significant contrast to Burke, however, Tocqueville refused to let this aesthetic category break out of its proper confines and take on political ramifications.

A brief comparison of Tocqueville's and Burke's ideas on the correct relation between politics and aesthetics will make this difference clear. To begin the comparison, a concise outline of Burke's doctrine of the sublime is in order.

The sublime is an aesthetic category that Burke uses to refer to those circumstances, scenes, or events that give rise to a paralyzing awe and terror in the soul of the beholder. It is associated with the ideas of pain and danger and with the individualistic instinct of self-preservation. He opposes the sublime to a category that contrasts with it in every way: the beautiful. Our awareness of beauty derives from the generative instinct and corresponds to the social domain of love and pleasure. Of the two, the passions that erupt in conditions of pain and danger are much more powerful than the social passions: "Whatever is fitted to excite the ideas of pain and danger, that is to say, whatever is in any sort terrible, or is conversant about terrible objects, or operates in a manner analagous to terror, is a source of the *sublime*; that is, it is productive of the strongest emotion which the mind is capable of feeling. . . . The ideas of pain are much more powerful than those which enter on the part of pleasure."[14]

The two categories have distinct gender-based connotations. The principle of beauty, associated with the feminine virtue of sympathy, stands in danger of being violated by sublime, masculine ambition. And while the regular, smooth, polished characteristics of beautiful objects are treated as feminine qualities, the traits of the sublime—vast, rugged, and asymmetrical—are seen as masculine.

Finally, and most significant, Burke's sublime has important political implications, for crucial to sublimity is a fearful consciousness of the presence of overmastering power. "Pain is always inflicted by a power in some way superior, because we never submit to pain willingly" (*W*, 139). One leading Burke scholar, Burleigh Taylor Wilkins, gives the political interpretation of this passage: "[Government] can be socially useful and can occasion feelings of pleasure, but it can be a creature of destruction capable of giving more pain than it could ever give pleasure. The energies of government must, therefore, be held in check and used with restraint."[15] In a more recent analysis, Bruce James Smith is more direct. "Burke's politics," Smith writes, "can be seen as an effort to recast the state in maternal categories"[16]—that is to say, because mothers are beautiful and fathers sublime, Burke held that the task of politics is to feminize authority, or counteract the sublime with the beautiful.

To Burke, the French Revolution was a horrible epitome of the political sublime: an act of parricide and regicide, the revolution attempted to strip away the obscure veil of hallowed, unquestioned tradition and custom that chastely envelops political and social authority.

The final point (for our limited purpose) about sublimity's effect is the paralysis it inflicts on the awestruck soul, which in the grip of its passion thus becomes a sort of antithesis of the sublime scene's potency. Sublime emotions pervade the soul completely and bring all its operations to a standstill. "The passion caused by the great and sublime in *nature*, when those causes operate most powerfully, is astonishment: and astonishment is that state of the soul in which all its motions are suspended, with some degree of horror. In this case the mind is so entirely filled with its object, that it cannot entertain any other, nor by consequence reason on that object which employs it" (*W*, 130).

This soul-filling experience is also fundamental to understanding Tocqueville's confrontation with the sublime spectacles of the New World's wilderness.

At the very outset of the *Democracy*, Tocqueville makes a revealing and unexpected observation to the reader. "This whole book has been written under the impulse of a kind of religious dread inspired by contemplation of this irresistible revolution" (*DIA*, 16). The reference to religious terror would have been familiar to most of Tocqueville's readers in 1835, the year the first volume of *Democracy in America* reached English and American booksellers. The 1830s witnessed the apogee of a certain kind of romantic sublime in both life and discourse. It was the age of *le romantisme social*. From Emerson's *Nature* to Delacroix's *Liberty* and the revolution it immortalized, to Berlioz's *Symphonie funèbre et triomphale*, one encounters everywhere the images of terror, awe, destruction, and vastness.

Yet locating Tocqueville chiefly among the Romantics, however inevitable the connections between his rhetoric and that of his contemporaries, would be misleading, for he always made a great point of being a dispassionate social scientist. Such avowals are scattered throughout not only the *Democracy* but also his other published works. Even on so provocative a subject as slavery, an evil to which he would return more than once in his public career and which he passionately believed had to be eliminated, he would argue chiefly and in almost ostentatiously neutral language about its economic disadvantages. And of the *Democracy* he said, "This book is not precisely suited to anybody's taste. . . . I have tried to see not differently but further than any party" (*DIA*, 20).

So the rhetoric of the sublime makes only a fleeting appearance in Tocqueville's published work and, therefore, might be dismissed as a fashionable turn of phrase. But ample evidence exists, in the notebooks and diaries left unpublished during his lifetime, that the conventions of the sublime and the emotions with which they were associated were a good deal more significant to him than his published *oeuvre* indicated. Evidence of the sublime and its attendant emotional states is especially abundant in Tocqueville's writings about nature and the wilderness. A comparison of the sublime in Tocqueville and Burke demonstrates, however, that the former was much more careful not to view politics in ways that evoke aesthetic experiences. Such circumspection on Tocqueville's part stems from deep convictions, convictions that had become firmly rooted in his soul before he ever left France in that spring of 1831.

Two texts are central to this examination. Both were drafted in 1831, during the American journey, and later revised and polished, but neither was published during Tocqueville's lifetime. The first, "Journey to Lake Oneida," is an altogether remarkable vignette concerning a side trip Tocqueville and Beaumont made from Syracuse to the marshy shores of this glacial lake and thence by rowboat to a glorified sandbar known locally by the intriguing name of Frenchman's Island. Beaumont published it in his edition of Tocqueville's *Oeuvres complètes* in 1861. The second text is the longer and somewhat less rapturous "A Fortnight in the Wilds," which Beaumont caused to be printed in the *Revue des Deux Mondes* in 1860.[17] It tells the story of the two adventurers' audacious journey to and beyond the verge of civilization—to the shoddy and miniscule settlement of Saginaw near the shores of Lake Huron. These works show a tendency to alternate between a swooning surrender to emotion and a lucid antiromantic practicality, with the former characteristic dominant in the Oneida essay and the latter in "A Fortnight."

Tocqueville and Beaumont worked hard to reach Lake Oneida, driven by the memory of a story they had been familiar with from the Old World, which told of "a young Frenchman and his wife, driven from their country by the storms of our first revolution." The couple found their refuge in the heart of the wilderness, the island of Tocqueville and Beaumont's destination, and there "lived for one another." The story, Tocqueville recounted, "left a deep and lasting impression . . . [it] always remained in my memory" (*J*, 345).[18]

Plunging into the endless forest, the two exiles from the next generation's revolution feel its "sombre savage majesty [that] fills the soul with a sort of religious terror" (*J*, 343). Just what evoked that sublime response? It was the riotous chaos of life and death randomly intermingled. "The air seemed impregnated with the smell of vegetation." Dead and decaying trees stood athwart their path while among "these immobile corpses" thousands of plants crept and wound. "It is like a fight between death and life." Amid the awesome solitude, the two friends walked for hours on the way to the shore, "our souls filled with the grandeur and the novelty of the sight" (*J*, 344). Eventually they reached the scene of the two exiles' bittersweet consolations, where deep under the vines they uncovered traces of a cabin and even an aged apple tree. Their hearts being, as he says for the third time, "full of emotion" and "inspired by some sort of a religious feeling" (*J*, 348), they undertook the return journey to the mainland.

There is more to this delightful and affecting essay than first appears, however. Clearly, the works of his uncle's brother Chateaubriand, author of *Atala* and *René*, whose romantic depictions of the American wilderness had all Europe swooning in Tocqueville's early youth, were in Tocqueville's mind.[19] But beneath its rather conventional comparisons of nature and civilization, life and death, exile and home, here, as in all of Tocqueville's writings, is an unmistakable sincerity. Tocqueville is never dishonest, and we would be wrong to dismiss this short piece, as even G. W. Pierson did, as an indulgence in a romantic divertissement by two somewhat playful youngsters.[20] On this point, Tocqueville himself stepped outside his narrator's role to speak in a different voice. "Perhaps those who read these lines will not understand the feelings they record," he wrote. "Nonetheless I will say that it was with hearts full of emotion" that the expedition was concluded.

Still more revealing are the notes from which the essay was composed. "Sight wonderful and impossible to describe," he wrote in his little pocket notebook. "Astonishing vegetation. Enormous trees of all species. A disorder of grasses, plants, bushes." Of the island itself he jotted: "With difficulty we reached the island. Emotion we felt on setting foot there." And finally, most revealing, the notebook entry ends with these words: "This expedition is what has most vividly interested and moved me, not only since I have been in America, but since I have been travelling" (*J*, 128).

Our sense of the import of this notebook entry is underscored when we consider the long, sobering, yet in places humorous "A Fortnight in the Wilds," written just three weeks after the Lake Oneida essay. Leaving Syracuse, Tocqueville and Beaumont journeyed along the route of the newly opened Erie Canal to Buffalo, where they boarded a steamboat that carried them the breadth of Lake Erie to "a little town of two or three thousand souls" (*J*, 358)—Detroit; from there they embarked on a genuinely risky excursion through the Michigan wilderness to Saginaw. Once again the awesome wilderness filled their souls. "I came to the banks of the stream," Tocqueville recalled, "and could not forbear stopping a few minutes in admiration of the sublime horror of the scene" (*J*, 377), and went on to describe its immensity, darkness, silence, and solitude. The following day, too, brought its intimations of horror. In the Michigan wilderness, as in the region of Lake Oneida, nature presented an appalling wild exuberance of life and death. "Offshoots, creepers, and plants of every sort press across every obstacle to the light. They ramp along the trunks of fallen trees, they push their way into the rotten wood, and they lift and break the bark still covering them. Life and death meet here face to face, as if they wished to mingle and confuse their labours" (*J*, 382). At noon the woods are pervaded by "a silence so deep, a stillness so complete, that the soul is invaded by a kind of religious terror" (*J*, 383).

"A Fortnight in the Wilds," however, conveys undercurrents of quotidian practicality that serve to undercut the sublime emotions. This essay is also a bitter satire and critique of the hard-edged, calculating American—of the beautifully drawn tavernkeeper, for example, who, although he would gladly undergo weeks of hardship in the appalling wilderness for the sake of a few dollars' profit, cannot comprehend the motivation of two foreigners who wish to enter the forests to experience their beauty. In fact, Tocqueville and Beaumont were driven to pose as prospective buyers of land in order to obtain directions. The entire, seemingly boundless region of forest, stretching from Detroit to the

Pacific Ocean, was, Tocqueville knew, just awaiting its despoliation. The American pioneer represents "the race to whom the future of the new world belongs, a restless, calculating, adventurous race which sets coldly about deeds that can only be explained by the fire of passion, and which trades in everything, not excluding even morality and religion. . . . [It] shuts itself up in the solitudes of America with an axe and a newspaper, . . . [showing] a scorn of life which one could call heroic, if that word were properly used of anything but the strivings of virtue" (*J*, 364). In his "vast egotism," Tocqueville scathingly notes, the pioneer seems to regard even his wife and children as "a detached part of himself" (*J*, 363). Surrounded by unsurpassed natural landscapes, yet unaffected by them, these grim and unfeeling Americans help to disclose the artificial character of the sublime. Tocqueville's notebook contains this entry, under the heading "National Character of the American": "The American . . . is only accustomed to change and ends by looking on it as the natural state of man. Much more, he feels the need of it, he loves it, for instability instead of causing disasters for him, seems only to bring forth wonders around him" (*J*, 187).

Although sublimity seems at times to overawe the travelers, then, the presence in the wilds of such a species as this Yankee pioneer subtly alters Tocqueville's conception of the destiny of this wild country. At last the contrast is made explicit in a passage linking the American wilderness to the nineteenth century's conventional literary symbol of sublime feeling, the Alps. "I have been through terrifying solitudes in the Alps, . . . where even in its very horror the sheer grandeur of the scene has something that transports one's soul with excitement." In North America, by contrast, "everything, as in Milton's *Paradise*, is ready to receive man" (*J*, 372), and one feels rather a gentle melancholy. Thus, Tocqueville is ultimately ambivalent about the sublimity of the American wilderness.

It is difficult to establish how much of Burke Tocqueville had read before his travels. Certainly he read deeply in Burke later in his life. As one would expect, Tocqueville's *The Old Regime and the French Revolution* contains many references to Burke.[21] But Tocqueville's familiarity with English writings began in his early twenties. He wrote a long and discerning essay on English history at 23. It seems certain that Tocqueville, a prize-winning student of rhetoric, had more than a passing familiarity with a Burkean vocabulary to express the depth of his emotion, but that before he had thoroughly grounded himself in Burke he had become aware of the dangers of being transported with emotion. This lesson is an important chapter in Tocqueville's intellectual biography, and contrasting Tocqueville with Burke is an illuminating way to approach it. Tocqueville always said he held three writers most dear: Montesquieu, Rousseau, and Pascal.[22] To the author of *Democracy in America*, the works of Montesquieu are clearly central and the subject of most commentary. The other two sides of the pyramid may seem at odds, but, in fact, the spirit of the romantic Rousseau and that of the Jansenist Pascal seem to balance each other. Tocqueville was always capable of deep emotion, but he seems to have learned early in life to repress it. He simply did not trust his emotional transports, hence the ambiguity concerning nature in "A Fortnight." Even on the shores of Frenchman's Island, where as he tells us he underwent a profound experience somehow linking death and life, he had enough presence of mind to jot in his notebook an acerbic sketch of Elam Lynds, a Syracuse businessman and the father of the controversial Sing-Sing prison (*J*, 126–27).

What kept Tocqueville from making a connection between the sublime and politics was the Pascalian, rather Jansenist, side of his personality. Imbued with the notion of life's fundamental seriousness, he also came to think of it as a struggle between deep emotion and dedication to duty. Just three months after his journey to Saginaw, Tocqueville wrote from Philadelphia to one of his most intimate friends in France, Charles Stoffels: "Like you, like all men, I feel within me an ardent passion that carries me away toward limitless happiness. . . . But that, you can be sure, is a foolish passion that must be fought. . . . Life is neither a pleasure nor a sorrow; it is a serious affair with which we are charged, and toward which our duty is to acquit ourselves as well as possible."[23]

At the end of "A Fortnight in the Wilds" occurs a sudden rush of a powerful, sublime memory "in the midst of that profound solitude." "I cannot describe the impact with which memories of July 29 took possession of our minds," Tocqueville recounted—for it was the first anniversary of the great revolution of 1830, soon to be immortalized by Delacroix. Indeed, Tocqueville's memory is a verbal correlative to Delacroix's great painting, *Liberty Leading the People*. "The cries and smoke of battle, the roar of guns, the rattle of rifles, the even more horrible ringing of the tocsin—that whole day with its delirious atmosphere, seemed suddenly to rise out of the past and to stand before me like a living picture." That day was also (although he does not mention the fact) Tocqueville's twenty-sixth birthday. Yet the combined effects of the two anniversaries are not sufficient to shake Tocqueville's knowledge that life is a serious affair. "When I raised my head and looked around me, the apparition had already vanished; but never had the silence of the forest seemed so icy, the shadows so sombre, the solitude so absolute" (*J*, 403).

Unlike the fiery Burke, Tocqueville had somehow learned that the sublime presented a false picture of life. Although the inward emotion is real enough, it has no correlative in the world of practical action. Indeed, it is precisely the tendency of sublime scenes to fill the soul and freeze its ability to reason that is the source of Tocqueville's caution. For him, the political sublime led to dispassionate appraisal, not—as it did for Burke—an upsurge of the instinct for self-preservation. As we have seen, Tocqueville did, in fact, feel sublime emotions when he contemplated the great revolutions of his own day. Yet—again unlike Burke—he saw in democracy's rise a phenomenon that could be disentangled from the tumultuous revolutionary scenes that so astounded Europe. In the closing pages of *Democracy in America*, he stressed this point for the benefit of readers who might have missed its earlier expressions. "I venture once more to repeat what I have already said or implied in several places in this book," he wrote. "One must be careful not to confuse the fact of equality with the revolution which succeeds in introducing it into the state of society and into the laws. In that lies the reason for almost all the phenomena which cause our surprise" (*DIA*, 688). It is this incomparable skill at distinguishing the sublime *emotion* from its *source*, a source that is in principle amenable to social scientific analysis, that to my mind establishes Tocqueville as the far greater social thinker than the incessantly outraged Burke.

Politician and Prophet

Tocqueville and Beaumont's trip to America was an exhausting, exhilarating experience for both. After visiting the Michigan wilderness, their itinerary took them to Montreal, Boston, and Philadelphia. Then they traveled down the Ohio and Mississippi Rivers to New Orleans in the worst winter ever recorded up to that time, surviving extreme cold in a Tennessee pioneer's cabin and a steamboat accident on the Mississippi. Finally they traveled overland across the militant South to Washington and Baltimore, and thence back to New York and the journey home. Wherever they went, they took every opportunity to inquire, to discuss, to solicit documents. "Tocqueville, when travelling, never rested," Beaumont recalled. "Rest was foreign to his nature; and whether his body were actively employed or not, his mind was always at work. . . . It never occurred to him to consider an excursion as an amusement, or conversation as relaxation. . . . For Tocqueville, the most agreeable conversation was that which was the most useful. The bad day was the day lost or ill-spent. The smallest loss of time was unpleasant to him."[24]

When they returned to France, however, Tocqueville's reserves of energy seemed to dissipate. The travelers' first obligation was to produce the report on prisons that had justified their journey. But Tocqueville's mind so teemed with the thoughts that he would soon organize into a coherent theory of democracy, that he simply could not write. Beaumont took on most of the actual composition of their joint work on prisons, which was published in 1833 and was a great critical success, receiving the Montyon Prize from the Académie Française.

In 1832, Beaumont, who was then busy writing *On the Penitentiary System*, was fired from his prosecutor's post for political reasons. In a gesture of solidarity, Tocqueville submitted a magnificent letter of resignation: "Having long been a close friend of the man who has just been afflicted with a dismissal, sharing his opinions and approving of his conduct, I feel I must voluntarily join him in his fate and, with him, abandon a career in which service and conscience cannot protect one from an unmerited disgrace."[25]

But, as might be expected, this resignation provided a kind of liberation, too. After a visit to England, probably to meet the parents of Mary Mottley (who had been raised by an aunt in Versailles, where Tocqueville met her), but also to make some observations about the society from which the United States had taken its "point of departure," Tocqueville set to work in an attic room in his parents' home on the rue de Verneuil in Paris. In one year he produced the first volume of his masterpiece. When it was published in January 1835, Tocqueville's life was changed forever. The venerable liberal theorist Pierre-Paul Royer-Collard called him the Montesquieu of the nineteenth century; across the Channel, John Stuart Mill wrote a long, admiring essay in the *London Review*. "The chief merit of it will be in the extracts," Mill generously wrote his new friend.[26] The book was at once translated into English by Henry Reeve and was an immediate international sensation.

So, when Tocqueville and Beaumont embarked on their second journey together in April 1835—this one to England and Ireland—Tocqueville was lionized. The highest reaches of London society strained to make his acquaintance, and he was invited to give testimony before a Parliamentary commission on corruption at elections. But, as before, the two friends remained conscious of their duties. Beaumont would harvest from this journey (and a second one he made in 1837) a two-volume work on Ireland, while Tocqueville's observations and notes would bear fruit in the second volume of *Democracy in America*.

After two months in London, the voyagers turned north, stopping in Birmingham, Manchester, and Liverpool, then crossed to Ireland, which they visited together for about six weeks. Tocqueville ran out of money and had to return to France in mid-August.[27] While the significance of Tocqueville's reflections on English politics and society for his emerging analysis of democracy are quite apparent, the full relevance of his shocked observations in Ireland are perhaps less appreciated. There he saw a civilized despotism come full circle to a condition of barbarism; it was to him the worn-out extremity of a despotic aristocracy. "If you wish to know what the spirit of conquest, religious hatred, combined with all the abuses of aristocracy without any of its advantages, can produce," he caustically observed in his notebook on 9 July 1835, "come to Ireland."[28]

On 26 October 1835, Tocqueville and Mary Mottley were wed in the church of Saint-Thomas-d'Aquin in Paris and in a few weeks were residing at the estate of his brother Edouard. When Alexis began work on the second volume of *Democracy in America* there, little did he know that nearly five years would pass before the work would be released to the public. Nor could he have known that during those five years the public itself would have changed and would receive this second volume in a spirit more of deference than of excitement.

In part, the delay derived from Tocqueville's political ambitions. For years he had envisioned a public career for himself, and now, with the success of his book and with his own ideas having achieved a high degree of clarity, he sought a seat in the Chamber of Deputies. Denied victory in his first campaign, in 1837, he was victorious in 1839, and never thereafter received less than 70 percent of the vote of his constituents for the remainder of the period of the July Monarchy and even beyond it to the first elections of the ill-fated Second Republic, in 1849. He would spend the decade as a highly respected, if not powerful, deputy from Valognes, a small city some 15 miles south of Cherbourg on the Cotentin peninsula, where the ancient family manor of the Tocquevilles, inherited by Alexis in 1836, was located.

One of the first assignments Tocqueville drew was to serve on a special committee appointed by the Chamber to investigate the abolition of slavery in the French colonies. The resulting report, composed by Tocqueville, is in fact a neglected classic of antislavery literature.[29] In it, he attempted not only to demonstrate how slavery was a moral abomination, but also how practically to come to grips with its extinction. The British had just completed an elaborate and awkward emancipation process, the morality of which was matched only by the clumsiness of its execution. All Europe was captivated by the British action. In his "Report on the Abolition of Slavery," Tocqueville advocated a kind of state socialism. France, he argued, should step in between the colonial planters and their bondservants during the abolition process, for which the planters would receive some compensation. Despite its combination of practicality and morality, the committee report, analyzed below, got nowhere in a political system seemingly designed for paralysis.

Tocqueville also took a strong stand on the emerging question of French imperialism and particularly the French occupation of Algeria. He was an enthusiastic supporter of the subjugation of non-European peoples, for, he reasoned, such invigorating actions would serve the dual purpose of shaking the French out of their political lethargy and advancing the cause of civilization among the unfortunate victims of barbaric despotism. In few places in the history of European liberalism is so glaring a contradiction evident than in this spectacle of liberty's great champion endorsing military subjugation in the name of national greatness. Unfortunately, in this as well as in his more uplifting calls, Tocqueville was a herald and exemplar of the modern condition.

The year 1840 saw the publication of the second (and, many believe, greater) volume of *Democracy in America,* also in its way a great public success. Tocqueville had received a second Montyon Prize for the first volume, plus an award of some 12,000 francs. He had been inducted into the Academy of Moral and Political Sciences. Then, on 23 December 1841, came the highest honor to which any French intellectual could aspire: membership among the 40 "immortals" of the Académie Française. And yet he was as restless as ever.

In May 1841, he embarked on a third journey with Beaumont, this time to Africa. The Algerian question seemed so pressing to him that he had to see the region firsthand, so that he could make a report to the Chamber on this great question as well. But the trip was a disaster that came to a premature conclusion when Tocqueville was felled by a paralyzing attack of dysentery. He had to be trundled to the coastal city of Philippeville in a donkey cart. There he awaited a ship to take him home. By early June he was back in France. The contents of his Algerian report were predictable in any event. Believing in the paramount importance of great deeds for a somnambulant nation, he did not hesitate to call the conquest the single most important question facing France.

Throughout his career in the Chamber, then, Tocqueville acted as a defender of liberty and a supporter of colonization. Those two principles were, to him, not only not in conflict, but capable of coexisting in serene harmony. He believed that there could be no liberty without political and social vitality, no vitality without greatness, and no greatness (at least at that moment of the nineteenth century) without colonies. Tzvetan Todorov's pitiless charge that "Tocqueville's colonialism is merely the international extension of his liberalism" is incontrovertible.[30]

Perhaps, Tocqueville thought, at one point in its history, France, like other nations, ought to have refrained from such a rapacious conquest. But because all other nations save France had expanded and because the conquest has commenced, it must be seen through. "Once we have committed that great *violence* of conquest, I believe we must not shrink from the smaller violences that are absolutely necessary to consolidate it." Furthermore, "any nation that readily lets go of what it has taken and withdraws peacefully of its own accord back inside its old boundaries proclaims that the golden age of its history is past. It visibly enters the period of its decline."[31]

By a peculiar set of circumstances, these principles led to the souring of his friendship with John Stuart Mill. In 1840, France found herself diplomatically isolated when, by the terms of the secret Treaty of London, England combined with those paragons of autocracy, Austria, Prussia, and Russia, to deal separately—that is, without regard to France—with the vexatious Muhammed Ali, pasha of Egypt. In so doing, they blocked French designs in North Africa. The French were outraged when the treaty provisions were revealed, and talk of war filled the Chamber and the salons. Tocqueville was fearful of new barriers being erected both to French expansion and French influence. He perceived in the pact between England and the autocracies a danger to the ideals of liberty and equality that France most vigorously represented in the world—a world increasingly imperiled by despotisms both old and new. In a fiery speech he condemned both the European governments' actions and the French government's response; then, in a tactless letter to Mill, he vented his anti-English prejudices, and the relationship never recovered.

Frustrated by the sterile policies of the two leading politicians of the July Monarchy, Adolphe Thiers and François Guizot, Tocqueville in 1844 purchased a controlling ownership of the newspaper *Le Commerce* and used it as a vehicle for the propagation of his own ideas. It was a lively paper, with regular contributions from the English radical Charles

Buller (who was asked to contribute only after Benjamin Disraeli polite-
ly turned down the offer), and, on American affairs, from Franz Lieber, a
liberal American immigrant intellectual who had translated *Le Système
pénitentiaire* and who was at that time a professor at the University of
South Carolina. The paper, however, failed to attract sufficient capital—
and subscribers—to keep it going, and failed by the summer of 1845.[32]
On 27 January 1848, Tocqueville rose in the Chamber to speak.
Immediately upon being recognized, however, he turned from the question before the deputies to address a quite different subject and delivered
one of the most famous speeches of the July Monarchy, if not of all of
French history.[33] What he said on that winter afternoon came to stand
as a symbolic counterpart to the *Democracy*'s many famous predictions,
and it probably did more than any event to establish Tocqueville's reputation as a prophet. Ironically, while the period of Louis Philippe was one
rich in parliamentary eloquence, Tocqueville himself shares none of the
glory for this ornament of the age. He was an uncertain speaker with a
hesitant delivery, acutely sensitive to his oratorical defects. But that day,
he warned of the coming of the great revolution of 1848 in a specific and
insistent way:

> Can you not see that little by little there are spreading among [the work-
> ing classes] opinions and ideas which are not concerned with just over-
> throwing this or that law, this or that administration, even this or that
> government, but society itself, shaking the very foundations on which it
> now rests? Do you not understand that they are constantly repeating
> that . . . the present distribution of property in the world is unjust? . . .
> Do you not believe that when such opinions take root, when they spread
> almost universally, when they go right down deep into the masses, they
> must sooner or later, I do not say when, I do not say how, but they must
> sooner or later lead to the most dreadful revolutions?
>   Such, gentlemen, is my profound conviction. I think that we are
> slumbering now on a volcano.[34]

Within a month, Paris was crisscrossed with barricades, King Louis
Philippe was in exile, and the monarchy was gone forever. Moreover, the
great uprising in Paris was but the prelude and prototype for similar
insurrections throughout Europe.
    France was suddenly a republic—though a doomed one—and
Tocqueville returned to the Cotentin to stand for election to the new
Chamber, this time under conditions of universal male suffrage. The
electors demonstrated great esteem and affection for their deputy, which

Tocqueville feelingly reciprocated. He was elected not only to the new legislature but also to the Constituent Assembly. He would have an opportunity to help construct the framework of the new government— to try to bring about a political regime that would avoid the democratic dangers to liberty he had been brooding about for two decades. In the debates, he advocated a bicameral legislature and a popularly elected president. He lost on the first point but won on the second.

Early in the course of the Constituent Assembly's deliberations, on 15 May 1848, their meeting place, the Palais Bourbon, was invaded by a throng of workers and radicals demanding support for Polish independence. "France [must] not sheath her sword until all Poland has been restored to her former boundaries!" cried the revolutionary orator and indefatigable conspirator, Louis Blanqui. And thus it was that, as the historian Georges Duveau wrote, "Behind the dream [of republican liberty] the towering image of Napoleon rose again."[35]

Tocqueville's dread of revolution is legendary, and fundamental to an understanding of his diagnosis of democracy. He hated and feared such an unleashing of anarchic forces. Revolution was for him a glaring symptom of a social state that lacked the desire and means for that ordered liberty that was the foundation of social progress. Thus, in his great memoir of the 1848–51 period, *Recollections*, written in 1850–51 while his memories were still fresh, he blends fiery scorn with incisive analysis in describing both the events of 15 May and the far more tragic devastation of the following month, when many of these same workers, desperate, hungry, and cheated, rose in armed rebellion against the Provisional Government. The workers were defeated utterly. Thousands were massacred, and hundreds of the survivors transported to Devil's Island. Tocqueville applauded this outcome, relieved that the forces of socialism had been unable to smother the infant republic in its gilded nursery.

The latent Bonapartism that Georges Duveau noted—the towering image behind the dream of freedom—became manifest all too swiftly. Louis Napoleon Bonaparte, nephew of the emperor, was elected the Second Republic's president in 1849. In the spring of that year, his prime minister called upon Tocqueville to serve as foreign minister, a position he filled with proficiency if not distinction for five months. In the unpredictable political atmosphere of the short-lived republic, ministries came and went with dizzying rapidity.

On 2 December 1851, the anniversary of the Battle of Austerlitz and of Napoleon's *coup d'état* of 1799, Louis Napoleon himself engineered a coup that destroyed the republic. Napoleon's nephew was now Emperor

Napoleon III, his bold seizure of power soon to be confirmed in a plebiscite by 92 percent of the voters. The despotism that Tocqueville had detected lurking behind France's desire for order at any cost displaced the republic. Tocqueville and a few courageous members of the Assembly opposed the coup; Tocqueville himself was arrested and even briefly imprisoned for his pains. In an act of audacious resistance, he arranged to have smuggled to England a scornful account of the coup and its aftermath, which was promptly published in the *London Times*.

But Tocqueville faced another kind of challenge in these years. In March 1850, he coughed up blood for the first time. In truth, the restless energy and appetite for physical challenges that Tocqueville had displayed during the trip to America were deceptive, disguising a constitutional fragility and susceptibility to illnesses. Several of his contemporaries remarked on his sickly appearance and frail build. "He was a small, slight man with an agreeable, regular, but sickly face," recalled Charles de Rémusat, who also noted "the livid pallor of his skin."[36] His coughing of blood was but the first definite sign of the tuberculosis that would claim him nine years later. Weakened almost to the point of immobility, he retreated to his château at Tocqueville in the summer of 1850, and there composed the first part of his memoir of the 1848 revolution. When autumn arrived, his alarmed physician strongly recommended his removal from the cold, damp air of Normandy, and the Tocquevilles departed France for a sojourn in Sorrento, where they could enjoy a view of Mount Vesuvius from the roof of their terrace. There Tocqueville continued work on his memoir, a book whose intimacy of tone reflects the concerns of a seriously ailing man of middle age. "These pages are to be a mirror," he wrote, "in which I can enjoy seeing my contemporaries and myself, not a painting for the public to view."[37]

Although the *Recollections* reveals a private perspective on Louis Bonaparte's seizure of power, Tocqueville also aspired to produce a broader historical interpretation. His restlessness, natural ambition, and sense of the fundamental seriousness of life all inclined him toward writing a quite different kind of book, a history that would uncover the deep-seated changes that had led to the calamity of Napoleon III. But, as R. R. Palmer observed, Tocqueville had a "tendency toward a kind of infinite regression in the focus of his efforts."[38] And so his desire to understand the coup of 1851 led him to the subject of Napoleon I, the great original more or less theatrically imitated by his own nephew; the consideration of Napoleon in turn directed him to the situation preceding the 1799 coup; from there he was inevitably steered to the French

Revolution; thence again to the state of France before the Revolution. Here Tocqueville could finally cease his regression, for in 1836 he had produced an essay on "The Social and Political Condition of France before and after 1789" for John Stuart Mill's *London and Westminster Review*. Building on this base, Tocqueville in 1853 began deep researches in primary sources in Tours, where he enjoyed the diligent assistance of a celebrated archivist, Charles de Grandmaison. He also traveled to Germany to study the structure of feudal society at its point of origin.

The result of these labors was *The Old Regime and the French Revolution* (1856), an abiding classic of historical literature. Despite the depth and range of the research that went into this book, however, Tocqueville brought his narrative only down to the inception of the French Revolution, reserving the analysis of that period to a projected later volume that he never finished. (He did leave considerable drafts and copious notes on the subject, which have since been organized by the editors of his complete works.)

This work's influential thesis is that the French Revolution had been accomplished long before the upheaval of 1789 or even 1787. The argument came as a revelation. Tocqueville's patient scholarship had unearthed a prerevolutionary France that was well along the path of the social and political changes that almost everyone had associated with the turmoil of the Revolution itself. Indeed, he had been arguing at least since the *Democracy* that a major historical confusion had resulted from people's failure to distinguish certain key social and political transformations—such as the advance of the doctrines of liberty and equality—from the revolutionary tumult that attended their triumph.

This second masterpiece was met with critical acclaim, as well. Indeed, when in 1857 Tocqueville made another journey to England, this time to gather materials in the British Museum for his second volume on the French Revolution, he was deluged with dinner invitations. He consistently declined such offers—including one from the Prime Minister himself, Lord Palmerston. (Of course, Tocqueville may have harbored an old grudge in this case because Palmerston, as foreign minister in 1840, had engineered the Treaty of London.) In a remarkable tribute to Tocqueville, the First Lord of the Admiralty arranged for a ship of the British fleet to convey him from Plymouth to Cherbourg at the close of his visit.

It was his last public triumph. The following spring, while in Paris trying to write, he saw with horror that he was coughing blood. "Eight years ago, a terrible illness had begun in the same way," he wrote to an

English friend.[39] As he had done eight years before, he remained in the north for the summer, but when the winter winds began to whistle through the cracked walls of the estate at Tocqueville, Monsieur and Madame de Tocqueville left for the warmer air of the south. From their cottage at Cannes, Tocqueville wrote the letter summoning Beaumont. Beaumont came, and stayed, and indeed left, just ten days before Tocqueville's death. In the last week, his cousin and intimate friend, Louis de Kergorlay, sat with him. He died on 16 April 1859.

Tocqueville and Modernity

One might contend that, when young Alexis experienced the panic of disenchantment in the library of his father's home in Metz, he was encountering a universal phenomenon. The disillusionment of the perceptive teenager who comes to doubt the existence of God, who suddenly fathoms the contingent nature of the social arrangements of his time and place, who sees through the veil of his society's exalted ideas and values while not ceasing to be moved by them: such a destabilizing awareness belongs, it would seem, in the early chapters of the biographies of sensitive adolescents throughout history.

But invoking this shibboleth of universalism as a way of understanding the significance of Tocqueville's disillusionment would be misleading. For, in fact, we effectively dismiss it and learn little by calling it universal. To the contrary, this experience of his was a limited one—representative not of all time but of modern times. Certainly the vast majority of all adolescents who ever lived never came to doubt God's existence or the universal validity of their society's values. Tocqueville described his experience in very specific terms. He called it a break between ideas and feelings, between the head and the heart. To comprehend the meaning of this rupture or split is to begin to understand Tocqueville's importance for us. For this rupture is exactly parallel to what Max Weber and others have persuasively argued is characteristic of the modern condition par excellence: "The increasing intellectualization and rationalization," Weber contended, ". . . means that principally there are no mysterious incalculable forces that come into play, but rather that one can, in principle, master all things by calculation. This means that the world is disenchanted."[40] He might almost have been describing Tocqueville's personal experience when he wrote in one of his most important essays: "The tension between religion and intellectual knowledge definitely comes to the fore wherever rational, empirical knowledge has consistent-

ly worked through to the disenchantment of the world and its transformation into a causal mechanism."[41]

But it not just "disenchantment" that, according to Weber, inevitably
attends the advance of scientific and technological control, of what he
called "instrumental reason"; it is also accompanied by the permanent
splitting of human concerns into separate "value-spheres" of truth, justice, and aesthetic value. "'Scientific' pleading is meaningless in principle
because the various value spheres of the world stand in irreconcilable
conflict with each other."[42] As one commentator on Weber explains,
"Prior to rationalization [in the Age of Enlightenment], questions of
truth, moral justice, and aesthetic value were not sharply distinguished.
Rather, they were treated as religious concerns resolvable by appeal to
the unitary will of God. . . . Rationalization changes all of this by eman-
cipating science, law, and art from religious dogma and grounding them
in distinct formal-rational procedures. . . . The internal development of
each of these *cultural value spheres* in turn issues in distinctly modern attitudes and institutions."[43] Part of the significance of Tocqueville's "sublime" experience in the forests of New York and Michigan was personal,
unique to him; but it is also important because it demonstrates his
recognition of the modern necessity of separating politics from aesthetics, power from beauty.

Weber's insight has been largely taken over by contemporary students of modernity, and his two touchstones of disenchantment and
separation are now seen as modernity's defining characteristics. As
Anthony J. Cascardi summarizes, an "overarching" theme of modernity
is "the splitting of the subject and the division of discourses": "The
modern subject is defined by its insertion into a series of separate value-
spheres, each one of which tends to exclude or attempts to assert its priority over the rest."[44]

The life and work of Alexis de Tocqueville present a singularly clear
example of this process near the moment when the separation of spheres
was beginning to occur, and we can observe its effects on a mind that
manifested great powers of insight and self-possession. Tocqueville, in
short, is that seemingly paradoxical combination, a classic modern—
someone who recognized and struggled to formulate for the first time
questions about liberty, democracy, revolution, and culture in such a way
as to allow us to recognize them as *our* questions. And the intellectual
power of this nineteenth-century voyager was, moreover, informed by a
moral seriousness, a love of freedom, and a beauty of expression that
place him in the ranks of his century's most compelling writers.

Still another factor that endows Tocqueville with the status of a classic modern is his persistent concern with the social problems of an emerging industrial society. Thus, not only were the intellectual and cultural pre-occupations of this new world filtered through and given expression by his singular intellect, but also, as Seymour Drescher first showed nearly a generation ago, the problems specific to "the transition from a preindustrial to an industrial society"—problems that social scientists broadly consider under the rubric of "modernization"—were probingly examined by him during the entire span of his public career.[45]

Tocqueville, then, is significant to us chiefly because he speaks to our modern condition. But there lies behind his modern concerns an antiquated sensibility derived from an aristocratic order, and this doubleness infuses his works with a rich multivalence. In Tocqueville nothing is unambiguous. Furthermore, although he addressed specific problems and conditions that were being created in the nineteenth century, Tocqueville viewed them as problems to be understood in light of concerns he thought were universal, however contingent and culture-bound we might consider them today. "I have only one passion, the love of liberty and human dignity," he wrote to his translator Henry Reeve. He went on with a compelling self-analysis that captures that sense of doubleness and lost unity. "I came into the world at the end of a long revolution, which, after having destroyed the old state, had created nothing durable. Aristocracy was already dead when I started life and democracy did not yet exist. . . . I was so thoroughly in equilibrium between the past and the future that I felt naturally and instinctively attracted toward neither the one nor the other."[46]

One of the most acute students of modernity, Jürgen Habermas, has written: "The term 'modern' again and again expresses the consciousness of an epoch that relates itself to the past of antiquity, in order to view itself as the result of a transition from the old to the new."[47] In Alexis de Tocqueville we can see one of the clearest examples of such a consciousness, linked to older, and indeed timeless, "universal," concerns.

Chapter Two

The Shape of Democracy:
Democracy in America, Volume One

Tocqueville as a Philosopher of History

"A modernity without models," writes the German philosopher Jürgen Habermas, "had to stabilize itself on the basis of the very diremptions it had wrought." Prominent among those "diremptions" (or divisions: *Entzweiungen*) was the one that emerged during the course of the nineteenth century as the new democratic forces wrenched themselves away from the firm structure of the old aristocratic society. For G. W. F. Hegel, to whom Habermas is specifically referring in this passage, philosophy was thus "confronted with the task of grasping *its own* time—and for him that means the modern age—in thought."[1]

When Hegel died, on 14 November 1831, 26-year-old Alexis de Tocqueville was in Philadelphia making preparations for the western portion of his American journey. The great task of grasping the modern age was the unashamed goal of the ambitious young Frenchman as well—one toward which he would make a stunning advance in the study that was already taking shape in his notebooks. For among the very few texts indispensable to the modern world's understanding of itself *as* modern, *Democracy in America* occupies a central place. In it, Tocqueville presented not just a portrait of a bustling, greedy, and prosaic new people, the "Anglo-Americans," but also a philosophy of history in which democracy serves as the defining characteristic of a new social formation. Democracy was—is—new in the world, yet it was absolutely fundamental to the future political and social state of the nations of the West.

Tocqueville can be called a philosopher of history because he offered cogent answers to the three questions that, according to William Dray, any speculative philosophy of history must confront: What, if any, is the pattern of the events of the past? What is the driving force behind those patterned events? And what meaning does human history have for us, given that it manifests the pattern and its driving force?[2] This chapter and the next present, if not a phenomenology, at least a careful walking tour through the *Democracy*, but it is a tour with a specific destination: an understanding of how Tocqueville viewed "the irresistible revolution" of advancing equality[3] as part of a vast historical process creating potentially irreconcilable diremptions. To take just one brief example, to which we must return later in the tour: in order to draw out the contrast between the national and state governments, Tocqueville had recourse to what I take to be the primary dichotomy in all his work, that between ideas and feelings. "The sovereignty of the Union is an abstract entity," he writes, "[whereas] the sovereignty of the states strikes every sense" (166). He elaborated upon the distinction by using the nature-culture opposition: "The sovereignty of the Union is a work of art. That of the states is natural" (167). Building upon this fundamental division (artifice-thought and nature-sense), Tocqueville would portray contrasting attitudes of remarkable complexity. As Tocqueville will explain, this difference between state and nation is one that arises from what he calls the Americans' "social state." The salient feature of that social state, in turn, is equality, and that condition of formal equality teems with contradictions.

Tocqueville's philosophy of history makes its appearance in a concentrated form in the "Author's Introduction" to the *Democracy*, an essay that Hugh Brogan has rightly called Tocqueville's "*credo*."[4] Tocqueville opens by recalling the force with which the fact of equality struck him during his travels in the United States. So great was equality's influence, he realized, that it permeates not only political life but civil society, customs, and the very emotions of Americans as well. Equality, he concludes, is "the creative element from which each particular fact derived" (9).

Then, in a maneuver that will come to characterize the rhetorical pattern of the entire book, Tocqueville shifts his attention from America to France and undertakes a rapid review of its history. Permeating this survey, imparting to it a strangely moving tone of dignified urgency, is the great theme of the interplay between human and divine agency. Echoing the narrative of the renowned François Guizot, whose course in European history at the Sorbonne he and Beaumont had followed with great excitement a year earlier, Tocqueville contends that, as the Middle Ages took shape, social relations in Europe became denser and more complex, civil society and mercantile boldness awakened, and the human mind began to exercise ever greater control over the blind hazards of a crude way of life.[5] The direction of French, and indeed of Western, history at this stage was one of increasing freedom from con-

tingency. Concomitant with this liberation from the vicissitudes of
nature were a slow decline in the powers of the aristocracy and a growing sense of empowerment among the people. Human agency and social
equality are thus woven together in this narrative of the great drama of
the emergence of Christendom from barbarism.

But, like the powers of the sorcerer's apprentice, or the forces of capitalism as Marx and Engels would describe them 13 years later, the forces
of equality, too, once awakened, themselves took on a force quite independent of the human intellect whence they had originated, a force that
was gaining ever greater momentum and threatening to overwhelm
man's powers of foresight and planning. Such a prospect—the loss of
human control over massive social, historical, or natural forces—was a
persistent theme in Tocqueville's life and work, one which recurs, for
example, in his antislavery writings, in his arguments with Gobineau
over the effect of race in human cultural development, and in his mem-
oirs of the revolution of 1848, as well as in the *Democracy*. What must be
fought for at all events, he believed, is the sense of agency, of the efficacious intervention of reason and will, in human affairs.

If social equality's origins lie in the human intellect, then, its destiny
seems to rest in the hands of God. Tocqueville presents its ineluctable
advance as "something fated," "beyond human control." Like a Godzilla
of former days, this "irresistible revolution" sweeps forward "century by
century over every obstacle and even now [goes] forward amid the ruins
it has itself created." For this reason opposition to *démocratie* "appears as a
fight against God Himself" (12). The clear trend of modern history is
one of increasing enervation, of a diminution of the power of human
beings to affect the course of events, and a correlative waxing of imper-
sonal social forces.

What then of human agency? Is Tocqueville a determinist, despair-
ing of mankind's ability to control the mighty tides of democratic leveling; or is he a religious philosopher who delivers himself up to the
ineffable providence of God; or perhaps a mythologizer, fashioning an
image of irresistible force in order to advance a particular political agen-
da?[6] In fact, he is none of these, but rather an alarmed observer of a
new kind of society that was just coming into existence in a haphazard
and wild manner. He contended that, although the advance of democracy itself may be destined, the uses to which it may be put are not.
Although equality is our unavoidable, common fate, the customs,
mores, and laws of a democratic society are yet to be fashioned. Thus,
the man who sets his face against democracy is a fool, but equally

thoughtless is the torpid fatalist who, sensing democracy's impending triumph, blinds himself to the continuing role of man's active intervention in the cause of reason and a civilized common life. This duality is what Tocqueville was referring to in his famous remark, "A new political science is needed for a world itself quite new" (12). This quite new Tocquevillian world, inevitable yet still formless, is Habermas's "modernity without models."

In addition to the uncertain relation between divine and human agency, a second and even more significant dichotomy is found in Tocqueville's introduction—that between feelings and ideas. This second pair of oppositions, chiefly psychological in character rather than historical, is nevertheless closely related to the antecedent problem of God's providence and humanity's ability to affect the course of historical development. Tocqueville clearly states that, while democracy arose out of the "life of the mind," of ideas, the domain of religion belongs to a separate sphere, that of sentiment or feeling. Indeed, the separation of those two aspects of the human spirit is itself the chief of the divisions brought about by the rise of equality in France: "That harmony which has been observed throughout history between the feelings and the ideas of men seems to have been destroyed" (16). As I read the *Democracy*, this is one of the most important sentences in the entire two volumes. To see why, one must investigate the relation between the two sets of oppositions—that is, between the feelings-ideas split and the larger divine-human dichotomy in which it is embedded.

While, as we have seen, Tocqueville ascribes the rise of democracy to the triumph of an idea, he thinks religion emerges from sentiment. When he notes the destruction of the harmony between feelings and ideas, then, he is at the same time commenting on the rift between democracy and religion. Religion in France, he contends, has "become entangled with those institutions which democracy overthrows" (16–17). The object of his investigation was not America but democracy: "I saw in America more than America; it was the shape of democracy itself which I sought" (17). What so arrested Tocqueville's attention in the United States was precisely the apparent conjunction—or the absence of a disjunction—between democracy and religion. American civilization "is the product . . . of two perfectly distinct elements which elsewhere have often been at war with one another but which in America it was somehow possible to incorporate into each other, forming a marvelous combination. I mean the *spirit of religion* and the *spirit of freedom*" (46–47). That, too, is why the United States exhibits "the results of the democratic revolution taking place among us, without experiencing the revolution itself" (18).

In sum, modernity has produced acute divisions, the most agonizing of which is that between the intellect and the emotions; that split, in turn, is projected onto the social world in the form of a war between freedom and religion. The United States, however, which has, through the accidents of history, been spared the upheaval which in France gave birth to *démocratie*, shows the effects of that wrenching process in a pure, almost clinical form. For Europe, as Habermas has argued, equilibrium would have to be dynamic, a stabilization paradoxically based on disjunctions. But in America, as Tocqueville knew by 1835, modernity might have a different face and democracy a more stable future because there it could advance with the sanction of religious authority.

Bernard Lonergan's characterization of the historian as one who perceives in any given historical moment that which is going forward is especially pertinent to Tocqueville's self-definition.[7] For him, the human drama of modernity had a trajectory that arced from the aristocratic, feudal past to the democratic future. At the apex of that arc, the French Revolution stands like a keystone. It marks the beginning of the modern travail, which is characterized by the most fundamental choice of the human condition—that between freedom and despotism.

Thus, human history has, for Tocqueville, a discernible direction, that from aristocracy to equality. But such a deduction is in itself inadequate to a philosophy of history. For historical explanations to be philosophical, they must also provide a coherent account of the motive forces behind that which is going forward. For Tocqueville, that account is more complex and subtle than it is for other social theorists who have tried to account for modernity. Marx, for instance, sees the motive force as class struggle, driven and intensified in turn by the contradictions of industrial capitalism, with its social mode of production and its private capturing of the fruits of that social process. Where Marx presents a strong account of both the direction and driving force of the modern world, however, he offers a weak response to the third question, that of significance or meaning. Tocqueville, by contrast, is emphatic concerning the direction of modern history and its meaning, but somewhat oblique as to the driving force. Still, his explanation of historical causation is both discernible and coherent. Unraveling the argument, one feels Tocqueville struggling with the deepest levels of historical explanation. If the results are not fully satisfying, they are at least immensely suggestive.

For Tocqueville, the driving force of equality is . . . equality. That is to say, once put into play, equality of conditions becomes itself a cause, influencing the depths of society and moving it forward inexorably toward the fateful choice that lies at the heart of modernity. Tocqueville abstracts the problem of historical causation, placing it in a general category he calls "the social state." This social state is not itself uncaused, but derives from a "point of departure." Because in history, as in all sciences, one must start somewhere, for practical purposes the point of departure for Americans lies in the fusion of the Puritan agony over salvation with the political freedom attendant upon the Puritans' exile to American shores in the seventeenth century. He insisted that "one should continually bear in mind this point of departure" when he made the decisive assertion that "Anglo-American civilization is the product . . . of . . . a marvelous combination [of] the *spirit of religion* and the *spirit of freedom*" (46–47).

These two "distinct but not contradictory tendencies," in turn, display their effects in two different spheres, namely mores and laws. As we might expect, the effects of the two engendering sources of the point of departure exist in an uneasy tension. "In the moral world everything is classified, coordinated, foreseen, and decided in advance. In the world of politics everything is in turmoil, contested, and uncertain" (47). And each exerts an uneven influence, custom ("the moral world") being more fundamental than law ("the world of politics").

The diremptions of *Democracy in America* are interrelated. Customs or mores (Tocqueville at first uses a number of interchangeable terms for this concept—*coutumes, usages, moeurs, habitudes*) are thus best understood as a consequence of the spiritual needs of man, subsumable under the rubric of feeling or sentiment, more closely tied to the feudal past, and derived from religious sources. The law, on the other hand, is the product of man's intellect, of ideas, and can be seen as an expression of the advance of democratic ideas and institutions. Thus it is that "the surface of American society is covered with a layer of democratic paint, but from time to time one can see the old aristocratic colors breaking through" (49).

These primeval mores and laws together thus constitute the point of departure for American civilization. But this point of departure gives rise to a condition even more generative than itself, namely the "social state." The social state serves in Tocqueville's analysis as an independent creative force, giving rise to the customs and laws that descend like neoplatonic emanations to a society, emanations appropriate to that particular society's point of departure. "Once [the social state] has come into being, it may itself be considered as the prime cause of most of the laws, customs, and ideas which control the nation's behavior; it modifies even those things which it does not cause" (50).

Its political consequences for the United States are predictable: rights are distributed to all. Its effect on customs and mores, what we might call its cultural consequences, are more complex and unsettling. The democratic social state results in a breakdown of the old laws of primogeniture, thus tending to cause both a more equal distribution of property—what Tocqueville calls the "direct physical effect of the law" of inheritance—and an "indirect" effect that extends "into the very soul of the landowner": the divorce of land from family feeling and its transformation into a commodity. Such consequences are paradigms of the cultural divisions that have come into being in the train of the democratic social state.

So there is in Tocqueville's *Democracy* a compelling and forcefully argued case for history's—or, better, modernity's—having a definite direction. It is the direction of equality, of social de-differentiation, and its roots lie in the febrile activity of the sphere of intelligence. Driving this historical juggernaut is the democratic social state, which itself is derived from a point of departure unique to each nation; for the Americans, that point is the Puritan past, with its paradoxical marriage of social rigidity and political individualism.

The significance of this historical panorama remains to be elucidated, but perhaps, given the foregoing analysis of Tocqueville's concerns, that significance might be inferred. Modernity has confronted the nations of the West with a stark choice. That choice is the dark and urgent theme that runs through the contrapuntal discussion of America and France: the alternative of freedom or despotism. For, in and of itself, *democracy is neutral in respect to freedom.* Tocqueville's whole life and public career, his triumphs and sometimes disastrous mistakes, arose out of the imperative need to shake France out of the periodic lethargy that had always led to barbaric despotism in the past. In the United States, the democratic culture seemed to hold out hope—it was by no means yet a demonstrated truth—for a future of liberty; but in France, which had left democracy "to its wild instincts," the prospects for despotism seemed much richer. Thus the significance of the march of the revolution of equality was world-historical. "It is a fearful problem concerning, not France alone, but the whole civilized world. If we can save ourselves, we shall at the same time save all the nations around us. If we fail, we shall bring them all down with us. According as we establish either democratic liberty or democratic tyranny, the fate of the world will be different" (xiv).

Modernity, then, presented to Tocqueville what, according to Habermas, it showed to Hegel as well: a legacy of torn, formerly compacted unities that have suffered through an irreversible process of diremptions. Head and heart, custom and law, sentiment and intellect, even liberty and despotism—all had been torn asunder from a prior unity. Because these rifts were irreparable, modern societies were faced with more, and more urgent, decisions than had been even remotely the case in the old aristocratic past. Man was free to be free—or to sink into despotism through a lethargy induced by that very freedom.

The Structure of *Democracy in America*

Democracy in America may be *formally* considered a meditation on an extended chain of causes and effects. The *matter* under consideration in this causal chain is equality of conditions. Its *locus* is the United States in actuality, and the entire Western world potentially, but especially France. Tocqueville's *aim* is to disclose both democracy's "hidden springs"— those ancient, glacially advancing social forces that cause its inevitable triumph—and its effects, the hitherto dim outlines of the possible future worlds that democracy will thrust upon humankind. His *method* is comparative, consisting chiefly of correlations among the United States, Great Britain, and France.

The work was published in two large volumes, five years apart, in 1835 and 1840. The 1966 English translation by George Lawrence runs to more than 700 pages. Each volume is divided into parts: volume 1 has two and volume 2 has four. While each of these six parts coheres, each is properly understood in relation to the whole work. Thus, the careful reader must retain her bearings by maintaining a sense of the terrain of the entire book. *Democracy in America* is eminently quotable and its plenitude of topics lends itself all too readily to the surgical zeal of the anthologist, but the full significance of its parts emerges only when the reader has journeyed through the whole. Before examining the argument of the work, then, it helps to be aware of its structure, a surprisingly neglected feature of most commentaries.[8] Accordingly, a brief survey of its contours is in order. The perspective from such a commanding height can be of great usefulness in fully comprehening the author's claims.

I have just referred to "an extended chain of causes and effects" as they relate to the subject of equality as the object under investigation. All such chains, however, must for practical purposes of human cognition start somewhere, must have a "point of departure." We know that democracy as it has developed in America has its point of departure in the remarkable fusion of "the *spirit of religion*" and "the *spirit of freedom*" that had been forged in the Puritan crucible. For Tocqueville, this harmonious amalgamation of feelings and ideas was of the first importance. He called his chapter on the subject "the germ of all that is to follow and the key to almost the whole work" (32). The point of departure thus has both a historical and a logical significance; that is, it operates as the opening scene of the narrative of the American story while at the same time logical consequences unfold from it as a premise.

After an eloquent first chapter in which he describes "The Physical Configuration of North America," Tocqueville goes on in chapter 2 of part 1 to disengage this point of departure from the surrounding inessential data and subject it to analysis. It henceforth functions as the prime cause, or first link in the extended chain. Tocqueville then proceeds to its major effect in chapter 3.

The combination of political freedom with religious piety had one consequence that overshadowed all others: the creation of a "social state" whose distinctive features were equality of conditions and social mobility: *démocratie*.

This democratic *social* state has had a specific *political* result, viz., "the principle of the sovereignty of the people" (58). "Now, I know of only two ways of making equality prevail in the political sphere; rights must be given either to every citizen or to nobody" (56). Considered in the abstract, the democratic social state might produce either result; there is no guarantee that equality will usher in a regime of rights. In the specific case of the United States, however, the former course, that of equal rights, has in fact obtained: rights are given "to every citizen." This principle of the people's sovereignty, although it is an "effect" of the social state, is itself a "cause" so fundamental that its living source will be considered at great length later in volume 1. But, at this point, Tocqueville introduces and defines it in chapter 4.

Finally, the principle of the sovereignty of the people has led to a particular "form of government" (61), and that form is the subject of Tocqueville's attention in the remainder of part 1 of volume 1 (chapters 5–8).

With the form of government that democracy gives rise to having been appraised, Tocqueville brings the first part of his masterwork to an ironic close. Remarking on the geographical isolation that, by immensely simplifying the problem of national security for the United States, has expedited the development of a federal system of government "favoring human prosperity and freedom," Tocqueville concludes: "To be happy and to be free [in the New World], it is enough to will it to be so" (170). Then the work begins its slow turn toward the analytical. Beginning with John Stuart Mill in 1840, most observers have recognized a more abstract, "philosophical" tenor to volume 2 of *Democracy in America*, but one might argue that, whatever the changed biographical and historical circumstances that may have led to the different emphasis so manifest in the second volume, there is also immanent within the structure of the work a philosophical turn that first emerges in the second part of volume 1. For here Tocqueville argues that behind, "above," "beyond" the "political society" that forms the subject of part 1 there hovers "a sovereign power": the people. The subject of part 2 is the people's "secret springs" (171). That philosophical process of going beyond surface appearances to explain the explanation—to show how, if the people's sovereignty constitutes the principle on which the political system is founded, the people themselves are motivated—is one that begins in the second half of the first volume.

In America, the people reign, but "the majority rules in the name of the people" (173). The people are depicted as a peaceful island surrounded by hectic agitation. The sources of this commotion are the parties, the focus of chapter 2. Political parties use two main weapons: newspapers, the "first of powers" after the people (186), and associations. Because volume 1 is concerned chiefly with the political consequences of the democratic social state, Tocqueville here treats the political repercussions of newspapers (chapter 3) and associations (chapter 4). (Later, in volume 2, the effects of newspapers and associations on civil society will be taken up [volume 2, part 2, chapters 5–7]).

After considering parties and their two chief instruments, Tocqueville's attention returns to the peaceful island, the people, and the question of how democratic government functions in practice, for "it is there [in the United States] that it must be judged," where "its features are natural and its movements free" (196)—not in France. Consequently, chapter 5, "Government by Democracy in America," is one of the most important in the entire work, not only for its impressive empirical content, but also for its extended comparison between American democracy and French aristocracy.

Democratic government has one matchless advantage: the continual agitation of political and civil life (chapter 6); and one paramount danger: the "omnipotence of the majority" (chapter 7), which may lead to tyranny. However, certain considerations serve to allay such fears and these are addressed next (chapter 8).

What one of *Democracy in America*'s most accomplished students calls "the true conclusion of the work,"[9] although it is not the final chapter, considers the factors that must be present for the maintenance of democratic government (chapter 9). Then, in a grim and famous chapter of almost 100 pages, Tocqueville concludes the 1835 volume with a brilliant essay on the "three races"—black, red, and white—who inhabit this tumultuous continent. Despite its auspicious pages of hope and expectation, volume 1 comes to a close on a tragic note.

Volume 2 of the *Democracy* was published in 1840 after agonizing delays had pushed its author increasingly behind his original timetable. The structure and content of this second volume will be considered in the next chapter. Here it is relevant to point out, however, that while the work as a whole concerns the causes and effects of the democratic social order, volume 2 pertains especially to its effects. Tocqueville's preface to the 1840 volume explains the distinctions in the aristocratic language of descent and progeny: "The democratic social order in America," he explains, "springs from some of their laws and conceptions of public morality"—those laws and mores that were the subject of volume 1. But something new is considered in the second volume, namely, the "new links" between persons, the fresh patterns of civil society, which are the "offspring" of this novel democratic order: "The book about American democracy which I published five years ago dealt with the first of these subjects. This book is concerned with the second" (417).

This distinction between progenitor and offspring is then deployed to underscore the different spheres of politics and civil society. Note, moreover, that civil society is the "offspring" of the political sphere of "laws and conceptions of public morality." For Tocqueville, politics engenders the distinctive institutions and patterns of thought and feelings that characterize a people's identity. Unlike Marx, he does not consider politics a mere reflection of the social imperatives determined by a particular mode of production, but rather, in the democratic context in particular, a vital, creative element.

Volume 1 is therefore, in the simplest, overarching terms, chiefly concerned with the origins and development of the democratic social state and of the ensuing dominion of equality. Volume 2 considers the effects (Tocqueville calls them "influences") of *démocratie*. Where volume 1 fixes its attention chiefly on politics, volume 2 focuses on civil society.

Volume One: The Argument

The Americans, Tocqueville says, "were the first to be faced with the above-mentioned alternatives" of freedom or despotism in a social state of equality, and "were lucky enough to escape absolute power" (57). For the next 100 pages and more of part 1, in his examination of the form of government, he explains how that was the case. (In part 2 he reveals why.) He commences with a detailed description of government within the states because "one must understand the state to gain the key to the rest" (61). The state comprises "three active centers, which could be compared to the various nervous centers that control the motions of the human body" (61): the township, the county, and the state itself.

Tocqueville's physiological metaphor is immediately connected to the theme—a persistent one in his works—of the distinction between civilization and barbarism. For the township is, by analogy to the lower-order functions of the nervous system, the governmental structure corresponding to the most primitive social arrangements. Townships are both archaic and universal—"coeval with humanity" and "rooted in nature" (62). The distinctive aspect of American townships is their freedom. Such liberty is everywhere "rare and fragile" (62), but virtually nonexistent in Europe, which is why it receives such patient attention from Tocqueville: "Among all the nations of continental Europe, one may say that there is not one that understand[s] communal liberty" (62).

Thus, although townships exist everywhere, free townships are to be found nowhere save in the United States. The township's "coarseness," its organic, wild qualities, make it especially vulnerable to the encroachments of the more centralized, efficient power centers of highly civilized societies. But in the United States, townships form the very sinews of the democratic social order.

The American township's autonomy is a direct consequence of the great political doctrine of the sovereignty of the people. Citizens in the townships defer to its authority not out of respect for a precept, however, but because they deem it to be in their interest. And the township itself is to the central government as the individual is to the township, that is, a free individual whose subordination is a matter of utility.

As has often been pointed out, Tocqueville took as his paradigm of the township, his Weberian "ideal type,"[10] the peculiar version he found and studied so assiduously in New England. He then generalized considerably from this somewhat localized example, defending himself with a hedge: "Townships and counties are not organized in the same way in all parts of the Union; nevertheless, one can easily see that throughout the Union more or less the same principles have guided the formation of both township and county. Now, I thought that in New England these principles had been carried further with more far-reaching results than elsewhere" (63).

In fact, however, as James T. Schleifer has discovered, Tocqueville examined the history and governmental structure of many of the states in the course of his construction of an ideal-typical township.[11] His singling out of Massachusetts as *exemplum* was thus the first of many illustrations of his method of "portray[ing] extreme states," as he termed it in an early draft of the work.[12]

Townships have come up with an ingenious solution to a fundamental problem of democratic social life. All societies "must submit to some authority without which they would relapse into anarchy" (72). Yet authority can easily overreach its bounds in the pretended interest of defending that very society, which is why Europeans tend to equate the establishing of liberty with the weakening of authority. The dilemma is that such a dilution of authority, while seeming to advance the autonomy of individuals, actually deprives society itself of certain rights that are legitimate. In the United States, administrative authority has been made to coexist with liberty by the simple expedient of subdividing the duties of administration and assigning each one to a separate town officer. "Functions can be multiplied and each man given enough authority to carry out his particular duty" (72); that is why "in a French commune there is really only one administrative officer . . . [while there are] at least nineteen in a New England township" (73). The *Democracy* abounds with such discoveries as this simple yet profound innovation in local administration.

An additional element serving to balance liberty and administration is the fact these diverse administrative functions never really intersect, for, strange though it may seem, each officer performs his separate duty without particular regard to those of his colleagues. Such coordination as may exist in this unusual system is due to the extension of the authority of the legislature, which, Tocqueville points out, perhaps somewhat wistfully, enjoys more latitude than is the case in France. Finally, the town officer himself is kept in check by both the judiciary and "a tribunal from which there is no appeal and which can suddenly reduce him to impotence" (78)—the votes of his fellow citizens.

Counties, the next level of authority (and complexity) after the townships, serve only a judicial function, the townships being too small to justify the expense of separate courts. "So, strictly speaking, the county has no real political existence" (71). Nevertheless, its authority increases in proportion to one's distance from paradigmatic New England, so that in Ohio and Pennsylvania, for example, "the county becomes the great administrative center and the intermediary between the government and the plain citizen" (81).

Before considering the central nervous system of the body politic (to pursue the metaphor that Tocqueville himself has by this time abandoned), the author raises an issue that henceforth will never be absent from his analysis of democracy: that of centralization. The question was especially vital to a native of France, where centralization had been a fact of such political importance for so long that its effects had permeated the very character of the French people.

We first encounter what may seem a puzzling distinction in the middle of a paragraph about the principles of administration: "The state rules," Tocqueville writes, "but does not administer" (82). Two pages later, in approaching the subject of the state, the third topic after towns and counties, he remarks: "I have spoken about the township and about administration; it remains to discuss the state and government" (84). While localities administer, then, states govern. Government and administration are different functions performed by different authorities. And both may be subject to the centralizing process.

> There are . . . two very distinct types of centralization, which need to be well understood.
>
> Certain interests, such as the enactment of general laws and the nation's relations with foreigners, are common to all parts of the nation. There are other interests of special concern to certain parts of the nation, such, for instance, as local enterprises.
>
> To concentrate all the former in the same place or under the same directing power is to establish what I call governmental centralization.
>
> To concentrate control of the latter in the same way is to establish what I call administrative centralization. (87)

Both government and administration, then, may become centralized, and in most instances that is what has taken place over time. When the two types of centralization combine, the consequences for freedom are calamitous. For the two kinds of centralization can fuse into a totalizing negation of liberty that leaves no room for individual autonomy. Then it is not only people's actions that are circumscribed, but their very feelings and thoughts as well. "Then," Tocqueville contends, "they are not only tamed by force, but their habits too are trained; they are isolated and then dropped one by one into the common mass" (87).

However, from what Tocqueville has learned about the system of local administration in America, with its segmentation of executive responsibilities, cheerful multiplication of magistrates, and unnerving electoral hazards, he concludes that the United States lacks *administrative* centralization. This distinction will prove to be of the highest importance for the subsequent analysis of equality and liberty. For the other, *governmental*, centralization exists in "a high degree" in the United States (89).

Tocqueville considers governmental centralization to be indispensable to national survival and prosperity. It becomes despotic when combined with centralized supervision over the minutiae of local life. The significance of such administrative control lies in its effects on the nature of public life: it fosters a debilitating lassitude, a kind of political enervation or lethargy among citizens whose capacity to exercise their volition thus shrivels to a vestige of its true potential for greatness. In keeping with a long European tradition, Tocqueville's model for such a political state was China. "Travelers tell us," he recounts, "that the Chinese have tranquillity without happiness, industry without progress, stability without strength, and material order without public morality. . . . I imagine that when China is opened to Europeans, they will find it the finest model of administrative centralization in the world" (91 n. 50).

Liberty, it would seem, must therefore be obtained at the expense of efficiency. "Freedom in a local community" is characterized by "numerous blunders," Tocqueville admits (62), while conceding too that "social resources would be more wisely and judiciously employed, if the administration of the whole country were concentrated in one pair of hands." The benefit of administrative decentralization, then, is not social or economic, but political: its very "blunders" and the absence of a commanding "pair of hands" provokes a kind of public agitation that, for Tocqueville, is the living manifestation of a society of free people. To drive home the point, he contrasts the "immaculate budget" and general "wretchedness" of the French commune to "those American townships, with their untidy budgets lacking all uniformity [and their] enlightened, active, and enterprising population" (93 n. 51).

Tocqueville is careful not to argue that European societies are doomed to tyranny by virtue of their administrative and governmental arrangements. What he does say is that aristocracies contain forces that are ever ready to combine in the face of such a threat. The example of the United States is pertinent precisely because it has no aristocratic past; its present is thus the West's future. As aristocracy declines, the seemingly banal details of public administration will take on a pivotal importance. If the nobility passes into oblivion as a political force, and if both administrative and governmental centralization endure, the prospects for despotism will be propitious indeed.

Another source of the balanced liberty the Americans seemed to nurture could be found in the role of their judges. Alexis de Tocqueville, juge auditeur of the Versailles courts, thoroughly trained and experienced in the procedures and principles of France's legal system, was keenly attuned to the unique position of judges, lawyers, and courts in maintaining the American "form of government."[13] The lawyer in Tocqueville was clearly fascinated with the judicial arrangements in the American "confederation," and he took pains to clarify what he candidly admitted was "the hardest thing there for a foreigner to understand" (99).

The difficulty for foreign observers arises from the superficial similarity, the seeming family resemblance, of the role of the judiciary in the United States and in Europe. As is the case everywhere else, judges in America are arbitrators; they decide particular cases rather than abstract precepts; and they may act only upon petition. To the uninitiated observer, then, the American judge seems quite familiar. And yet, in contrast to their role in European society, judges in America possess enormous political power. Given the similarity in formal roles between European and American judges, determining how this could be so is difficult. Tocqueville's trained eye, however, detected the crucial difference in the American system. It lay in the simple fact that "the Americans have given their judges the right to base their decisions on the *Constitution* rather than on the *laws*" (100–101). And this fact, in turn, points to the fundamental and unique role played by the Constitution, a subject Tocqueville will meticulously examine in the long chapter that closes the first part of volume 1.

In his analysis of the "judicial power," Tocqueville provides a classic instance of his comparative method, juxtaposing the American with the

French and British constitutions in an exercise perhaps more notable for its neatness than its subtlety. On the one hand is presented the supposedly unalterable French constitution, under which, precisely on account of that immutability, judges lack the power to pronounce on the constitutionality of the laws. The constitution of England, on the other hand, is subject to Parliamentary modification, making acts of Parliament constitutional by definition, and thus immune from judicial declarations as to their conformity with the fundamental law. But "neither of these two arguments applies to America." While the American, like the French, constitution cannot be modified by legislation in the English manner, it can be amended by the people, thus "reduc[ing] the judges to obedience. . . . So on this point," as Tocqueville discovers, "politics and logic agree" (102).

Another striking feature of American legality is the accountability of public officials to citizens, not simply by means of the electoral process, but also through legal prosecution. Tocqueville professed to find it impossible to explain to Americans the shocking immunity from prosecution enjoyed by public officials in France, a provision that emerged unscathed from the constitutional revisions that followed its original appearance in the Napoleonic Constitution of the Year VIII (1800).

Finally, Tocqueville notes a variance in American and European practice with respect to "political jurisdiction"—what Americans are familiar with as impeachment proceedings. The European counterpart to impeachment is a direct application of the criminal law to the alleged wrongdoer, while impeachment proceedings in the United States terminate with the removal of the offender from office. This observation leads to the remarkable insight that impeachment is "an administrative act which has been clothed in the solemnity of a judgment" (108).

Tocqueville's pleasure in analyzing the American judicial system is evident on every page. It gives this portion of the work a perhaps unanticipated vibrancy. Later, in volume 2, he discusses the subject of lawyers as a cultural phenomenon with a perspicacity equal to that in his treatment of the political role of judges in volume 1.

Part 1 concludes with what Tocqueville terms "a quick look at the federal Constitution" (112)—it occupies 59 close-packed pages in the Lawrence edition—that, after a few general remarks, follows the structure of the constitution itself, discussing first the legislative, and then the executive and judicial branches. In Tocqueville's view, not surprisingly considering the foregoing discussion of the "judicial power," the Supreme Court occupied the pivotal position between the competing forces of state and nation. And, again as might be anticipated, he discusses these forces in terms of the previously established categories of government and administration. While the federal government was established for certain clear and general purposes, the states' responsibilities are detailed and local in character. Because the founders knew that "in practice questions would arise" about the distribution of authority, "they created a federal Supreme Court" (115), whose influence and reputation Tocqueville would consistently overstate.

The ensuing précis of the constitution is necessarily somewhat dry, given the unfamiliarity of Tocqueville's French audience with the subject. Nevertheless, it is studded with keen observations that cast light on the concrete functioning of the political structure that had emerged from the democratic social state. For example, in a passage contrasting the scope and purpose of the powers of the president with those of the French king under the July Monarchy, he notes the importance of public opinion to both, despite the multitude of contrasts in their positions as executives; but, he adds, "in America it works through elections and decrees, in France by revolutions" (124). The contrast could hardly be more important to this proponent of "aristocratic liberalism"[14] whose life was, as Jean-Claude Lamberti succinctly reminded us, shaped by "love of liberty and hatred of revolution,"[15] and whose writings constitute a long and nuanced contrast between the two distinctive types of *démocratie* that emerge from revolution and from a social state of equality.

Again, Tocqueville, like James Madison before him, whom he had read with great care, emphasized the distinctiveness of the American constitution by drawing attention to the way in which the federal government had direct authority to enforce its own laws. "The Americans who united in 1789 agreed not only that the federal government should dictate the laws but that it should itself see to their execution." This constituted "one of the great discoveries of political science in our age" (156), because all "confederations" prior to the United States had left it to the provincial governments to execute the laws of the central authority.

The American constitution is distinctive, too, in that its benefits are not such as could be enjoyed by other nations. The reason for this singularity lies in the Americans' mores. Because the federal government is a complex contrivance, an "abstract entity" (166), its functioning demands a high level of comprehension from citizens, who must accept "the complication of the means it employs."

"[W]hen one examines the Constitution of the United States . . . it is frightening to see how much diverse knowledge and discernment it assumes on the part of the governed. The government of the Union rests almost entirely on legal fictions. The Union is an ideal nation which exists, so to say, only in men's minds" (164). But "nothing has made me admire the good sense and practical intelligence of the Americans more than the way they avoid the innumerable difficulties deriving from their federal Constitution" (165).

The second inherent weakness of the federal government derives also from that "abstract" quality. "The sovereignty of the Union is an abstract entity. . . . The sovereignty of the states strikes every sense" (167). The Union, associated in Tocqueville's prose with art, contrivance, abstraction, and fiction, contrasts somewhat frighteningly with the states, affiliated as they are with nature, feeling, and sensation. No people can be relied upon to exercise its reasoning capacity at all times; men and women are moved by the simple and familiar—by the local. In the United States, mores step in to fill the gap between reason and feeling, guiding the people to an accommodation between the general and the particular and causing the federal system to become assimilated in people's minds with a deeply felt but parochial patriotism that could be annoying to sophisticated transatlantic visitors. "The Americans carry national pride to an altogether excessive length," the irritated traveler jotted in his notebook on 15 May 1831. "Generally speaking there is a lot of *small-town* pettiness in their makeup" (*J*, 289–90).

Yet these people constitute an "almighty power" (171) that holds absolute sway over the laws and institutions of the nation. One reason Tocqueville's inquiry achieved the renown it did was because he peered beyond the surface of institutional structures to their sociocultural foundations—and in "the sovereignty of the people" he believed he had discerned those foundations.

The almighty people, however, are constantly assaulted by the supplications of the political parties. Having departed for America from Europe's most turbulent nation only months after France's third revolution in as many decades and having arrived only three years after organized parties made their appearance in Jacksonian America, Tocqueville understood the phenomenon of political parties only fitfully. He formulated a distinction between great and small parties, according to which the former dispute with one another over fundamental principles of government, while the latter quarrel over petty issues of local and selfish interest. Small parties are "without political faith. . . . They glow with a factitious zeal; their language is violent, but their progress is timid and uncertain," while great parties "have nobler features" because they are attached to principles (175). Such great parties, he continues, cannot be discovered in the United States, although they were to be found in the heroic generation that followed the American Revolution.

These parties are the most important beneficiaries of America's freedom of the press. Tocqueville's aristocratic sensibility was affronted by the 1830s counterpart of today's supermarket check-out journalism, but, in his own terms, he "love[d]" the liberty from which such trash could spring (180). He valued freedom of the press not for itself but for its results. Those ubiquitous and sometimes vile sheets make "political life circulate in every corner of that vast land. [The press's] eyes are never shut, and it lays bare the secret shifts of politics, forcing public figures in turn to appear before the tribunal of opinion" (186). And its power is enormous, owing, in all likelihood, to the very violence and vulgarity of journalistic discourse.

Freedom of the press is one of two instruments wielded by the parties. The other is freedom of association. Tocqueville's remarks on association are among the most sagacious and widely cited in the *Democracy* and, with the chapter on the press, form a diptych portraying the lineaments of free political action in a democratic nation.

Of the two, freedom of the press is the more fundamental; it is "the principal and, so to say, the constitutive element in freedom" (191). Liberty is thus constituted by the free use of language; indeed, associations might be said to be gatherings of men and women who support particular forms of interpretation.

In typical fashion, Tocqueville constructed a taxonomy of associations, the most elemental being a group tied by an intellectual bond to some doctrine. Following this in complexity is an association with nodes of activity in several regions, while the most advanced form is a national party with elected representatives and a political structure that mirrors that of the nation at large.

The benefits of free associations are manifold. They implant in the feelings and intellects of their members an affection for and experience in making use of their freedom. Thus, governments would be mistaken to restrict their activities except in severe circumstances. Most important, however, associations obstruct the otherwise unfettered will of the majority. For, once a political party emerges victorious in a democracy—and this was especially the case in Jacksonian America—it packs all public offices with its own supporters and blocks all avenues to power. Only the power of associations, exercised through the freedom of the press and assembly, serves to restrain the victorious forces. Thus, the multiplication of associations, considered by the classical theorists to constitute an evil because it signifies disunity in the body politic, actually serves a useful purpose in a democratic context.

But the associations characteristic of democracy differed from those of aristocratic nations in one crucial respect: they were not natural; they were, as with so much else in a democratic context, the result of artifice, and hence required discipline, skill, and especially the force of custom for their effectiveness. "In aristocratic nations," Tocqueville argued, "secondary bodies form natural associations which hold abuses of power in check. In countries where such associations do not exist, if private people did not artificially and temporarily create something like them, I see no other dike to hold back tyranny" (192). Such a contrast of nature and artifice, we have noted, permeates Tocqueville's interpretation of democracy, and has implications for much more than his theory of association.

The chapters on freedom of the press and of political association (volume 1, part 2, chapters 3 and 4) illustrate a number of Tocqueville's other preoccupations as well. First is his attentiveness to disclosure, to uncovering what lies beneath the surface; in this case, journalism's "lay[ing] bare" of the forces behind political transitions. Second is his reliance on the comparative method, by which political or cultural customs in France illuminate otherwise obscure American practices (for example, when Tocqueville contends that the press in America, for all its impact, has less influence than in France, where it is centralized and freedom of expression is a recent attainment). And finally, there is his double-sided concern with freedom and agitation. Tocqueville might even be said to define freedom as agitation within limits. For at one extreme, political commotion can slide over into chaos, signifying revolution; while at the other there lurks the despotism born of lassitude.

But distinctions between art and nature, civilization and barbarism, are even more fundamental to Tocqueville's analysis of democratic government. "Democratic government, founded on such a simple and natural idea [the sovereignty of the people], nevertheless always assumes the existence of a very civilized and knowledgeable society. At first glance it might be supposed to belong to the earliest ages of the world, but looking closer, one soon discovers that it could only have come last" (208). In volume 2 he was to write: "I think that in the dawning centuries of democracy individual independence and local liberties will always be the products of art. Centralized government will be the natural thing" (674). The modern, civilized epoch, then, is democracy's childhood, and as such calls for the artful application of human intelligence rather than unthinking instinct. In short, *liberty is an art*, never more so than in democratic eras. As Henry Steele Commager has written: "In the Old World . . . Nature had triumphed over Art. But in America, Art— by which Tocqueville meant intelligence, inventiveness, imagination, skill—might still contain or reverse the dictates of Nature."[16]

The discussion of parties and associations was a prelude to the heart of volume 1, the analysis of democratic government. Nowhere in the first volume does Tocqueville betray so intense a consciousness of his duality of purpose—"describing America and thinking of France"[17]—as in these troubled pages: "I know that I am now treading on live cinders. Every word . . . must in some respect offend the various parties dividing my country. Nevertheless, I shall say all I think" (196).

An adequate comprehension of Tocqueville's approach to the workings of democratic government depends, I believe, on the recognition of the premise that I have been trying to tease out of the context he has been slowly constructing throughout the book. We have seen the repeated reference to the art-nature polarity, as well as the observation that democracy occurs only in "very civilized and knowledgeable" circumstances. This means that successful—that is, nondespotic—democratic government is a product of the civilized arts. But now comes the added judgment that, in America, democracy is "natural and its movements free" (196). It is natural precisely because it lacks the aristocratic historical burden of the European states: democratic government was latent in the American point of departure, while in Europe it had to be established by means of the violent overthrow of the preceding social state.[18] Thus, democracy in America is at once civilized and natural; or, in other terms, in the United States, the art of democratic government is natural. American politics thus seems to share that "middle ground" between wilderness and sophistication that, Leo Marx found, the literature and painting of the emerging national culture occupied as well.[19] The "instincts" of democracy, in the New World, are not primitive, but advanced, uniquely modern ones.

For example, Tocqueville famously observed that the quality of statesmanship in the United States was declining with the advance of democracy, a deterioration he attributed to envy, that "secret instinct leading the lower classes to keep their superiors as far as possible from the direction of affairs" (198). Envy is a democratic, not a uniquely American, instinct; but in the United States certain laws, "democratic in their nature" (200), partially compensate for this tendency, such as the frequency of elections and the indirect election of the Senate (until 1914 senators were elected by state legislatures).

Again, American democracy manifests a frugal "instinct" in the payment of its high officials, and, in fact, the government as a whole is quite parsimonious. But this frugality arises out of the meager circumstances of private life. "If the Americans have never spent the people's money on public festivities, that is not only because there the people vote the taxes but also because the people have no taste for enjoying themselves" (215).

More important than these ruminations on envy or frugality, however, is Tocqueville's discussion of patriotism, which also turns on this same contrast between art and nature. The dichotomy this time is presented as an "instinctive" patriotism that accompanies love for home, ancestors, and tradition, on the one hand, and a "rational," "reflective" understanding of the complementarity of public and private well-being, on the other. The political associations of each type are explicitly drawn: "the instinctive patriotism of a monarchy" and "the reflective patriotism of a republic" (236). This latter sort of patriotism, republican though it may be, is plainly absent in the United States. It is the patriotism of the classical republics based on virtue, of which Tocqueville's master Montesquieu wrote. In the New World, however, neither politics nor patriotism emerges from virtue. In truth, American patriotism, like American democracy itself, is something altogether new. There the people recognize that "individual interest is linked to that of the country, for disinterested patriotism [that is, classical republican virtue] has fled beyond recall" (236).

Thus, the Americans' "irritable patriotism" (237) reflects neither the virtuous altruism of the classical republics nor the sentimental honor of feudal aristocracy but rather an attitude rooted in selfish calculation. Yet, *pace* Montesquieu, the modern sort of unvirtuous democratic government can avoid despotism by ensuring the widest distribution of political and property rights, thereby "linking the idea of rights to personal interest" (239). In this new kind of republic, virtue may be superseded by interest and live to tell about it.

This dispersal of rights helps to produce that agitation, that "restless activity" or "sort of tumult" (244, 242) that is the antithesis of the political and civil immobility of despotism. Moreover, the agitation of political life passes into and invigorates civil society itself. Indeed, Tocqueville says, "That is the greatest advantage of democratic government" (243).

Conversely, its greatest disadvantage is "the omnipotence of the majority." The greatest danger of the majority's rule, Tocqueville said, was a despotism derived from its hegemony over thought: "Under the absolute government of a single man, despotism, to reach the soul, clumsily struck at the body, and the soul, escaping from such blows, rose gloriously above it; but in democratic republics that is not at all how tyranny behaves; it leaves the body alone and goes straight for the soul" (255). This "tyranny" can, however, be limited. Its restriction is partly a function—and here we see the art-nature dichotomy come full circle— of the fact that, while the majority has "a despot's tastes and instincts, [it] lacks the most improved instruments of tyranny" (262). In other words, "it is only aware of its *natural* strength, ignorant of how *art* might increase its scope" (263, emphasis added).

But the most effective counterforce to the tyranny of the majority is the American legal system. One might argue that the nineteenth century's most impassioned opponent of despotism sought and found the guarantee of democratic liberty in the mirror. Certainly Tocqueville invested great hopes in the profession that had shaped him. His faith in lawyers arose from the conviction, discussed earlier, that aristocratic societies "naturally" contain forces that act as counterweights to tyranny. He perceived in the membership of the legal guild the shadow of an aristocracy amidst the democratic tumult. "Hidden at the bottom of a lawyer's soul," he observes, "one finds some of the tastes and habits of an aristocracy" (264).

In addition to the nation's attorneys, its judges, too, obstruct the democratic tide, as Tocqueville pointed out in his discussion of the judicial system. Finally, juries, a "form of the sovereignty of the people" (273), serve to educate citizens in the principles of the law. "The jury is both the most effective way of establishing the people's rule and the most efficient way of teaching them how to rule" (276). Here again Tocqueville saw that what he called the "defects" of democratic government could be remedied by supporting institutions or customs immanent in the democratic social state, rather than by erecting or defending anachronistic ones that are external and antithetical to it.

The single most striking aspect of democratic government in the United States, however, was its continuity: what needed explaining was not that it was established but that it endured. In a long chapter that seems to distill the main themes of the work, Tocqueville undertakes to explain that continuity. Deploying his familiar, artificial but somehow curiously illuminating taxonomic approach to explanation, he fits "the causes tending to maintain a democratic republic in the United States . . . into three categories" (277): circumstances, which he calls "accidental or providential causes"; laws; and habits and mores. Among today's historians, these factors would probably be considered to have been listed in

rank order of causation, for by circumstances Tocqueville meant the
ensemble of the physical and geographical environment, while by habits
and mores he intended the customary way of life of the people. The
overwhelming tendency of the social sciences since Tocqueville's day has
been to regard such mores as products of deep-seated social and environ-
mental influences. To Tocqueville, however, "the laws contribute more to
the maintenance of the democratic republic in the United States than do
the physical circumstances of the country, and mores do more than the
laws" (305). Indeed, he continues, the demonstration of that thesis is
"the main object of my work" (308). Once again habit and custom are
the reason the Americans' democratic government seems so natural,
while that of the French is compared to the behavior of a savage.

It is not, of course, a matter of these peculiar customs and mores
floating like Platonic ideas in the American air. As we recall from the
opening chapters, customs and habits originate in the social state
spawned by the point of departure unique to each nation. But once they
are generated, these customs and habits "control the nation's behavior"
(50). In the United States, two of these *moeurs* are particularly salient:
religion and "practical experience" generally (301).

The discussion of mores, like so much else in this simultaneously per-
spicacious and exasperating book, contains deep wisdom mixed with
inaccurate reporting and murky prognostication. But one element of
Tocqueville's discussion of this absolutely pivotal concept needs further
elucidation, especially after its use in a widely celebrated and moving
book that took Tocqueville as its own point of departure. In their 1985
study of American mores, *Habits of the Heart*, Robert Bellah and his coau-
thors took their title and indeed their theme—"individualism and commitment in American life"—from Tocqueville.[20] While Tocqueville did
refer to mores as "habits of the heart," however, he did not stop there: "I
here mean the term 'mores' (*moeurs*) to have its original Latin meaning; I
mean it to apply not only to '*moeurs*' in the strict sense, which might be
called the habits of the heart, but also to the different notions possessed
by men, the various opinions current among them, and the sum of ideas
that shape mental habits. So I use the word to cover the whole moral
and intellectual state of a people" (287).

It is essential, then, that we recognize mores not as matters of the
heart only but also of the head. The intellect as well as the passions
shapes American habits, and, given Tocqueville's association of democracy with reason in the opening pages of the "Author's Introduction," we
would be mistaken to associate democratic habits with feelings only. The

importance of this extension of the definition will become fully apparent only in the second volume, however.

Yet the heart holds one key to the maintenance if not the origin of democracy, for the heart, as Tocqueville saw things, was the domain of religion. While it is hard to disagree with Perry Miller's opinion that Tocqueville's pages on religion are "probably the least perceptive he ever wrote,"[21] they nevertheless provide the basis of a comparison between American and French democracy that may paradoxically be related to their shortcomings as reportage.

Religion possessed a political importance for Tocqueville far greater than for any of his contemporaries. He believed it to function as yet another of the barriers, this time an inward, psychological one, against the danger of social disintegration unleashed by democracy's potentially unlimited horizon. "While the law allows the American people to do everything," he says in a typical overstatement, "there are things which religion prevents them from imagining and forbids them to dare" (292).

In his presentation of the American "point of departure," Tocqueville had portrayed the Puritan world as a paradoxical combination of rigid mores and infinitely elastic politics. While the Puritan moral universe was fixed, "classified, coordinated, foreseen, and decided in advance," the political world was "in turmoil, contested, and uncertain" (47). This ambivalence continued to affect Americans' behavior in the Age of Jackson, he found, with the fluidity of politics being counterbalanced by the fixity of Christian dogma, so that "the human spirit never sees an unlimited field before itself" (292). Religion serves to rein in desire and discipline wants. "Despotism may be able to do without faith," Tocqueville concluded, "but freedom cannot." For "how could society escape destruction if, when political ties are relaxed, moral ties are not tightened?" (294).

This is "the true conclusion" of volume 1—a book that sees the future as unalterably democratic, but potentially either free or despotic, and that sees the only hope for freedom in the mores of the people. France, the subtext of the first volume, emerges to the surface in the second. The question there will be one of mores and civil society: given that France cannot and—thank God—ought not replicate American customs, what habits of heart and mind should be nurtured there to elude the despot's grasp?

Chapter Three

Head and Heart in a Regime of Equality: *Democracy in America*, Volume Two

A Scorn of Forms

Tocqueville opens volume 2 with great aplomb. He grasped the historic truths, now become clichés, that the story of modern philosophy begins with René Descartes (1596–1650), and that Descartes's influence on all modern thought can hardly be exaggerated. At the threshold of modernity, the enigmatic half-smile of this urbane gatekeeper (rendered so masterfully in the celebrated portrait by Frans Hals) must have aroused a curious mixture of self-confidence and apprehension in the mind of the earnest wayfarer seeking to understand the social and intellectual revolutions of the modern world. For on the one hand, Descartes is the ancestor of that "ground-clearing" tribe of philosophers that includes thinkers otherwise so different from him as Locke, Kant, and Rousseau. His fundamental message is that the past can be discarded because the rules for seeking truth are inscribed on the blueprint of every individual's consciousness. On the other hand, however, the very independence of thought such a supposed capability confers on each person can become a burden so enormous that he or she may shrink from intellectual life entirely in the belief that it is a vain undertaking and altogether not worth the effort.

For these very reasons, Tocqueville considered Americans to be the world's Cartesians par excellence. And, with an irony applicable in equal measure to America and Descartes, he remarked that their Cartesianism stemmed from a perfect ignorance of philosophy in general and of Descartes in particular. In a scintillating passage replete with punning allusions to Descartes's works, Tocqueville begins volume 2 by describing the "philosophical method" of the Americans: "To seek by themselves and in themselves for the only reason for things, . . . looking through forms to the basis of things. " In this nation where "each man is narrowly shut up in himself," he believed, "each American relies on individual effort and judgment. So, of all countries in the world, America is the one in which the precepts of Descartes are least studied and best followed" (429, 430).

Cartesianism is the specifically *democratic* philosophical method, Tocqueville says, and it severs the bond between generations even as it rends social connections. Cartesianism serves as a crucial link—the master link, really—in that extended chain of causes and effects Tocqueville is analyzing. That is why Jean-Claude Lamberti misleads us somewhat when in his clear and wise book on the *Democracy* he claims that the opening to volume 2 is "the true introduction to the work" as a whole,[1] for Cartesianism is itself an effect of the democratic social state that had been analyzed in the first volume. It is, however, also a cause, a kind of secondary "point of departure." It constitutes the conceptual foundation of the second volume, which will treat of the ideas and feelings created by *démocratie* and their effects, in turn, on mores and politics.

Ideas and feelings, mores and politics: these are the four categories Tocqueville analyzes in the four parts of volume 2. The book thus has a simple, straightforward structure. In part 1, "Influence of Democracy on the Intellectual Movements in the United States," the subject is intellectual life, whereas part 2, "The Influence of Democracy on the Sentiments of the Americans," is a study of how equality affects the emotions. In these two parts, Tocqueville contends that the democratic social state has profound effects that seep into the very souls of the society's inhabitants. This process of internalization can be seen, with sufficient distance, to conform to a pattern. This pattern, in turn, becomes a sort of template he imposes on the intellectual and emotional lives of democratic citizens. The abstraction, rather than the concrete details of America's political institutions, then becomes the subject of the work. It was apparently this very shift toward abstraction that made the second volume somewhat less engaging to readers of the 1840s, who had taken such delight in the specificity with which Tocqueville had rendered American society in the previous volume.

These ideas and feelings, products of a new kind of social state, in turn have profound effects on civil society. In part 3, "Influence of Democracy on Mores Properly So Called," Tocqueville examines the ways that, in the new society, "new links have been formed," and a new "pattern of civil society" has emerged (417). Finally, in part 4, "On the Influence of Democratic Ideas and Feelings on Political Society," he

shows how the new ideas and feelings affect politics. Volume 2, then, is
a study of intellectual life, of emotional life, and of the impact of these
first on customs and then on politics.

Thus does this decade-long project come full circle. Having begun
with a "point of departure" that linked politics with religion *ab origine* in
Puritan Massachusetts, Tocqueville ends by examining the politics that
issued forth, with many intervening links, from that archaic, yet also
modern, Puritan combination.

That the democratic head and heart will be the subject of volume 2 is
made especially clear in the author's preface, in which Tocqueville
explains that the new democratic social order whose genesis he had
chronicled in 1835 gives rise to what he first calls "feelings and points of
view," then "inclinations and ideas," and finally "feelings and ideas":
"The ground I wish to cover . . . includes the greater part of the feelings
and ideas which are responsible for the changed state of the world" (417,
418). And the general name he chose for those feelings and ideas was
Cartesianism.

Such a label, which, it must be acknowledged, would not pass muster
on an undergraduate philosophy exam, nevertheless represents a
sociopsychological insight of the first order. For what it indicates is that
individualism (a term Tocqueville did not invent but one he succeeded in
defining with a hitherto unmatched precision in part 2, chapter 2) is a
genuine "social fact"[2] with discernible effects on personality, civil society,
and politics. By using the term in this way, Tocqueville takes Cartesian
thought out of the seminar rooms and shows the concrete effects of ideas
on action.

The unschooled Cartesianism of the Americans, Tocqueville says,
"leads to other mental habits," and in particular to what he called "a
scorn of forms" (430), meaning by forms all the inessential social and
intellectual trappings, the rituals, conventions, and routines that obscure
one's vision and fetter the mind in its effort to attain a clear and distinct
idea of its object.

The Cartesian method being not strictly American but democratic,
however, it is also present in Europe insofar as Europe has experienced
social leveling. Indeed, in Europe it is much more extreme, and so the
scorn of forms can be observed there, as well.

Therefore, "let us turn our attention to the chronological development" of modern European thought, Tocqueville writes (430), and in so
doing inaugurates the shift of attention away from America and toward
France, which is a distinctive mark of the volume. The second point he

makes about the Americans' unconscious philosophical method is that it is susceptible to restriction. There are brakes on American Cartesianism. In France, by contrast, it is applied "more often and more strictly" (431–32).

The two restraints on American Cartesianism go to the heart of Tocqueville's concerns for the future of liberty in a democratic context. First, "it was religion that gave birth to the English colonies in America. One must never forget that" (432). Christianity saves Americans the wearisome mental effort of seeking first principles. And besides obviating metaphysics, its universal acceptance places most issues of morality beyond serious debate. Second, American democracy was established without revolution. The French, revolutionary, and turbulent kind of Cartesianism must therefore be distinguished from its circumscribed American counterpart. Once more, unique American conditions, which may not be transferable to France, afford reason to believe that democracy need not spawn anarchy.

But, under conditions that drive each person to decide for himself every question that arises, how does everyday life proceed? Everyone knows that, in practice, "rely[ing] on individual . . . judgement" whenever a decision has to be made is impossible. People need dogma—general ideas that are accepted unquestioningly: "it can never happen that there are no dogmatic beliefs, that is to say, opinions which men take on trust without discussion" (433). What is the source of such dogmatic authority if, as Tocqueville would have it, the whole society is Cartesian? The answer, as simple as it is menacing, is public opinion. Men and women simply absorb most of their opinions from the society around them. Thus is yet another Tocquevillian paradox put forward: "Democracy might extinguish that freedom of the mind which a democratic social condition favors" (436). This is another example of a dubious inference based almost entirely on a generalization, this time a generalization about Cartesianism rather than on empirical examination. But in defense of Tocqueville, it can be emphasized that the generalization is a deliberately radicalized "ideal type" or heuristic device by which to discern democracy's true "shape" and to separate its essential from its accidental features.

For Tocqueville, then, Cartesianism signifies the American penchant for generalization, for the grand inference. Americans make such deductions all the time, and this tendency is the single most important source of the shallowness of their intellectual life. For the "passion for generalization" Americans exhibit is of a singular kind: "It is important to make a distinction between different kinds of generalization. One kind results from the slow, detailed, and conscientious labor of the mind, and that kind widens the sphere of human knowledge. The other kind springs up at once from the first quick exercise of the wits and begets only very superficial and uncertain notions" (440). And it is this latter sort, in which intuition and instinct substitute for patient intellectual labor, that Tocqueville found among Americans.

Before leaving the subject of Cartesian speculation, Tocqueville elaborates on the role of practical experience and of religion in modifying the "excessive taste" (442) for conjecture that equality nurtures. "Practical attention" to the commonplace problems of life in a democratic community forces citizens "to go into details, and the details will show them the weak points in the theory" (442); while religion serves to discipline the potentially unlimited desires against the lure of which the souls of men are otherwise defenseless. He also observed with approval the purification of belief in the deity, rather than His agents, that equality sustains.

Tocqueville's analysis of religion is itself a curious blend of the speculation he so distrusts with down-to-earth, utilitarian calculation. In his anxiety about limiting desires, then, he projected onto Christianity the role of redeemer of one of mankind's temporal regimes, democracy: "The main business of religions," he cavalierly generalizes, "is to purify, control, and restrain that excessive and exclusive taste for well-being which men acquire in times of equality" (448).

The argument as presented thus far comprises only five chapters of the first part of volume 2. I have devoted disproportionate space to this subject of Cartesianism because of its disproportionate importance to the subject at hand, namely the workings of the hearts and minds of democratic citizens. While an understanding of its pivotal place in the argument is essential to Tocqueville's enterprise, however, the actual merits of the Cartesian thesis are surely questionable. Tocqueville seemed to believe that if his task—describing "the shape of democracy itself" (17)—could be accomplished, evidence contrary to his generalizations could be dismissed, not as false, but as accidental features of the landscape rather than essential components of it. Others have argued, however, that the seemingly "accidental" traits he discounted were much closer to being central truths, and that in pursuing his "ideal type" he missed important attributes of both America and democracy.[3] The understated complaint in the *Encyclopedia Britannica*'s ninth edition about "an excess of the deductive spirit" in Tocqueville's masterwork was as justified as it was elegant.[4]

Having introduced the subject of religion in this context of general ideas and democratic instincts, Tocqueville devotes two more short, pointed chapters on the subject, chapters that reveal once more how brilliantly penetrating he could be in some of his conjectures—and how outlandish others can seem when inspected under the unforgiving light of history. In the outlandish category is his prophecy that, because Catholicism best fit the criteria he had sketched about belief, ritual, and duty in chapter 5, "it would suddenly make great conquests" (450). On the other hand, in a cogent chapter titled "What Causes Democratic Nations to Incline Toward Pantheism," Tocqueville explains how, under conditions of equality, "the human mind seeks to embrace a multitude of different objects at once, and it constantly strives to link up a variety of consequences with a single cause. . . . [The democratic citizen] seeks to expand and simplify his conception by including God and the universe in one great whole" (451).

These seven chapters, with an eighth about the belief in the indefinite perfectibility of man, comprise a discrete section of the work. They are the indispensable source of illumination for the panorama of democratic beliefs and practices that is to come in the remainder, when he finally gets down to the previously announced business of discussing intellectual life, sentiments, civil society, and politics.

After this eight-chapter prologue, which comprises half of part 1, Tocqueville inserted a transitional chapter that discloses as clearly as anything in the volume his concern with France. To this point, Tocqueville had described Americans as unreflective, lacking in intellectual traditions, superficial, scornful of ceremony, and confined in the cage of public opinion. Now he takes great pains to explain why, although such baneful consequences may result from democracy in the United States, they need not be the fate of democratic peoples elsewhere. The chapter is important, then, not only because of the structural task it performs—that of a hinge between the strictly American and the broadly democratic—but also because in it Tocqueville contends that democracy need not foster barbarism.

Warning his readers against the danger of confusing "what is democratic with what is only American," Tocqueville offers three ways in which "the Americans are in an exceptional situation" when it comes to the national "aptitude or taste for science, literature, or the arts" (454, 455). First, he drags American Puritanism to the fore again, this time as a cultural rather than a political or social point of departure. The Puritans' austerity, scorn of liturgical forms, and depreciation of ceremony were inherently antagonistic to the development of art and literature. Second, the "breathless cupidity" (455) of this commercial society leaves no leisure for the life of the mind. Finally, the close American connection with the highly advanced civilization of Great Britain deprived the New World of the cultural inducements necessary to the forging of a vigorous, indigenous intellectual life. "We should therefore give up looking at all democratic peoples through American spectacles," Tocqueville concludes (456).

Tocqueville delivered these merciless judgments on the aridity of American intellectual life at the very moment that Ralph Waldo Emerson was composing his first great philosophical essays, "Nature" (1836), "The American Scholar" (1837), and "An Address Delivered Before the Senior Class in Divinity College, Cambridge" (1838). In scarcely more than a decade after *Democracy in America* was published, this allegedly shallow, greedy nation would experience that "flowering" of culture that has come to be known as the American Renaissance. The *Essays* of Emerson, Thoreau's *Walden*, Melville's *Moby-Dick*, Whitman's *Leaves of Grass*, the paintings of Fitzhugh Lane, William Sidney Mount, Albert Pinkham Ryder, and George Caleb Bingham—all these would soon burst forth in the great age, a true classical age, of American culture. It would seem, then, that Tocqueville's verdict on this count was less than just. Perhaps this is another example of his missing the trees as he tries to map the whole forest. Yet, in a curious way, his thoughts on this point echo those of Emerson himself, for in "The American Scholar" the Concord philosopher had drawn attention to precisely those features of America's democratic society that had stunted the development of the American intellect. Emerson was as sensitive as Tocqueville to the cultural dependency induced by European models of thought and discourse, and he called for a sturdy independence from the nurturing pieties of European culture.

Throughout the remainder of part 1, Tocqueville sometimes refers specifically to "the Americans" but more often alludes generally to "Democratic Peoples," "Democratic Centuries," or "Democratic Societies." Henceforth, Americans appear chiefly as foils or supplements to his judgments on European thought and feeling in democratic times. Tocqueville's survey of intellectual life spans many fields and institutions: the natural sciences, the visual arts, monuments, literature, language, poetry, oratory, theater, and history. (Interestingly, he has nothing to say in this analysis of "Intellectual Movements in the United States" about American colleges and universities.) His conclusions are everywhere alike: Americans, despite their inclination for general ideas, betray no penchant or appreciation for elevated thoughts or deeds but instead are drawn by nearly every social custom and institution toward the mundane and the useful: "His desires, needs, education, and circumstances," Tocqueville found, "all seem united to draw the American's mind earthward" (456).

What Tocqueville has put forward in these nine chapters, then, is a rather sophisticated two-tiered classification system, in which aristocracies are contrasted with democratic societies; and then, among the democracies, America with its primal "democratic social state" is differentiated from nations where equality was established through revolution. As Seymour Drescher demonstrated in an influential 1964 article, Tocqueville became increasingly concerned after 1835 about the lurching, uncertain progress of liberty in France. His focus in the second volume of the *Democracy* would therefore be on the problem of revolution and revolution's impact on a society with no rooted experience in widespread liberty.[5]

Tocqueville's instincts proved to be right. The United States experienced liberalism without revolution,[6] but in Tocqueville's France (and to some extent even today) liberalism was not always tied to democracy. The subsequent failure to disentangle these two strands of modern politics would torment France for decades to come. Theodore Zeldin might just as well have been writing the political history of Tocqueville's 1830s rather than the ecclesiastical history of the Third Republic (1870–1940) when he depicted antagonists "so carried away by the bitterness of their disagreements that they became incapable of understanding each other, and hopelessly confused as to what their quarrels were about."[7] It was precisely this confusion that Tocqueville recorded at the outset of his book, when he noted how in France "religion . . . has become entangled with those institutions which democracy overthrows" (16–17), whereas the United States benefited from an aboriginal fusion of "the *spirit of freedom*" and "the *spirit of religion.*"

Was it possible to reap the benefits of the revolutionary spirit—liberty *and* equality—without the anarchy that accompanied their establishment? Or must the future entail only the sinister alternatives of despotism or endless tumult? This is the essential problem posed by volume 2. Jean-Claude Lamberti characterizes it as "how to defend the values of 1789 while combating the revolutionary spirit,"[8] to which it may be added that those values encompass more than politics. Indeed, the task of this volume is to show how equality affects the sphere of culture as well as that of politics.

Logically, then, this concern with the effects of revolution appears on the first occasion in which the theory Tocqueville has been developing in those first nine chapters is applied. In chapter 10, on the Americans' preference for the practical over the theoretical in science (a proclivity, he says, that can be observed "among all democratic nations" [460]), he deploys his classification system to "make a clear distinction between the sort of permanent agitation characteristic of a peaceful and well-established democracy, and the tumultuous revolutionary movements that almost always go with the birth and development of a democracy" (460). The fact that French science astounded the world with great theoretical leaps at about the time of the French Revolution, he contends, ought to be ascribed "not to democracy but to the unexampled revolution which attended its growth," for the turbulence of revolution "cannot fail to give a sudden impulse to . . . feelings and thoughts." To attribute those advances in pure science to democracy, then, is to fail to disconnect the revolution from the democratic consequences it brought in its train. In fact, democracy as such, considered apart from revolution, predisposes scientists toward applied rather than pure research. After all, Tocqueville says, "nothing is less conducive to meditation than the setup of democratic society" (460). Consequently, "Nowadays the need is to keep men interested in theory" (464).

But Tocqueville's sense of a "need . . . to keep men interested in theory" derived from something much more important than the progress of pure science. As with everything else that was deeply important to him, he ascribed a political significance to it. For him, an aptitude for theory was actually a political necessity, because theory, in the sense of grand intellectual conceptions, can serve as a shield against despotism. We must not be deceived by the example of Rome, he contends at the end of this chapter, into believing that barbarians can only come from without. They can also develop within society and slowly darken the lights of civilization. For "confining ourselves to practice, we may lose sight of basic principles"—which is precisely what happened to that prototype of despotism, China. In that land, where a "strange immobility of mind" led the people to "drop the idea of improvement," to "copy their ancestors the whole time in everything," so that "human knowledge . . . almost dried up at the fount," science had expired (464). "We therefore should not console ourselves by thinking that the barbarians are still a long way off. Some people may let the torch be snatched from their hands, but others stamp it out themselves" (465).

This somewhat curious chapter on science, we can now see, functions as a paradigm. It occurs in the exact middle of part 1, after nine chapters that established a cultural theory adequate to the study of these strange new democratic times, and it sets the pattern for what is to come in all the areas in which that theory is to be applied. It is science, then, that offers the clearest picture of democratic cultural practices. Its built-in dialectic between abstract and practical, general and particular, appearance and reality, can be employed to illuminate art, literature, drama, and other "intellectual movements" in societies where aristocracy has been superseded.

And in all these cases, the pattern revealed by science will be repeated: the preference for the practical over the abstract, practice over theory, and the particular over the general will be shown repeatedly to be endemic to democracy. Thus, in the visual arts, "appearance counts for more than reality" (468); literature is "crawling with writers who look upon letters simply as a trade" (475); in the theater, "the pit often lays down the law for the boxes" (490).

Again Tocqueville takes pains to emphasize that these are democratic, not American, qualities. By this time, indeed, he has become completely detached from his American moorings. This book is not now about America at all. The critic of Cartesianism has become a Cartesian, left his ground, abandoned the concrete, and is writing about an abstraction. Tocqueville makes a revealing statement in this regard in a passage explaining the differences between the American and English versions of their common language. "Starting from a theoretical approach," he writes, "I came to the same conclusions that [certain experts] had reached empirically" (478). A more apt description of the method of volume 2 would be difficult to find.

The chapter on literature provides a good example. It is pointedly entitled "Literary Characteristics of Democratic Centuries," rather than of the United States, because "the Americans have not yet, properly speaking, got any literature," a fact he says is "not due to democracy alone [but] to peculiar and independent circumstances" (471). "By and large," he maintains, "the literature of a democracy will never exhibit the order, regularity, skill, and art characteristic of aristocratic literature; formal qualities will be neglected or actually despised [the "scorn of forms" again]. . . . There will be a rude and untutored vigor of thought with great variety and singular fecundity" (474).

But the aesthetic themes are not the only themes that will be repeated in the remainder of part 1. The political motif, the fear of Oriental despotism, which had appeared somewhat unexpectedly in the discussion of science, will also resurface in the ensuing analyses of democratic intellectual life. It shows through most clearly in a typically dogmatic pronouncement about history. If aristocracies generate histories emphasizing the heroic deeds of great individuals, Tocqueville maintains, historians in democratic times, "seeing the actors less and the events more," tend toward a deterministic interpretation of the past—a kind of fatalism. If this "doctrine of fatality" were to seep into the public consciousness, "it will soon paralyze the activities of modern society and bring Christians down to the level of Turks. . . . Such a doctrine is particularly dangerous at the present moment" (495–96).

Tocqueville's lifelong fixation on apathy and its political effects, then, shows up even in a discussion of historiography. It will shape his book even more forcefully in the subsequent sections on feeling, mores, and politics, until at last we are forced to recognize it as the true source and subject of this enormous ten-year enterprise.

The Love of Equality Itself

Turning to part 2, on the influence of democracy on feelings, one finds startling differences from part 1. If in the section on ideas Tocqueville had demonstrated an "excess of the deductive spirit," a tendency to favor the pontifical pronouncement over the factual assertion, and a confidence in his deductions that could border on the fatuous, in the second part he created one of the nineteenth century's greatest legacies to the future. In the profundity of its insights and its tone of ambivalence, even of tragedy, this discourse on the way equality transfigures the inner "sentiments" of persons in a democratic society helps give *Democracy in America* its status as one of the great modern texts.

"The first and liveliest of the passions inspired by equality is, I need not say, love of that equality itself" (503). Freedom and equality are poised on a scale that tilts with the contingencies of history. In democratic times, the scales incline toward equality. While freedom, not being "exclusively dependent on one social state," can be found in myriad times and places, "equality forms the distinctive characteristic" of democratic ages such as our own (504). It thus becomes "the ruling passion" that "seeps into every corner of the human heart, expands, and fills the whole" (505). And because these are democratic times, neither freedom nor despotism can be established without it.

Never one to forego a distinction, Tocqueville in chapter 2 introduces one that helps place his "sentiments" on a spectrum of inner sensation. The distinction he makes is that between individualism and egoism, and the variable on which the difference revolves is the degree of calculation that goes into each; or, conversely, the amount of instinct that each entails:

> Egoism is a passionate and exaggerated love of self which leads a man to think of all things in terms of himself and to prefer himself to all.
> Individualism is a calm and considered feeling which disposes each citizen to isolate himself from the mass of his fellows and withdraw into the circle of family and friends. . . .
> Egoism springs from a blind instinct; individualism is based on misguided judgment rather than depraved feeling. . . .
> Egoism is a vice as old as the world. It is not peculiar to one form of society more than another.
> Individualism is of democratic origin and threatens to grow as conditions get more equal. (506–7)

The differences are central to Tocqueville's understanding of democracy: egoism is passionate, instinctual, and primitive; individualism is calm, calculating, and modern.

We can see that individualism has been situated on a continuum of inner impressions at a location much closer to conscious "idea" than to subliminal "instinct"; it is a feeling at the margin of ideas. Consequently, Tocqueville coins various oxymorons to describe this new concept. It is a "considered feeling," he says, a kind of "enlightened egoism" (527). Egoism, in contrast, lies on the opposite edge, toward instinct: it is a "depraved feeling." The gamut of "sentiments," then, runs the entire distance between instincts and ideas, with egoism and individualism, despite their similarities, at opposite poles.

In 1840, individualism was a concept in the making. Tocqueville was the first political liberal to use the new term, which made its first appearance in a French dictionary only in 1836.[9] In the discarded drafts of 1840 that he called "Rubish [*sic*]," Tocqueville noted: "There are in *individualisme* two kinds of effects that should be well distinguished so that they can be dealt with separately. 1. *the moral effects*, hearts isolate themselves; 2. *the intellectual effects*, minds isolate themselves."[10] I have become convinced, however, that the reason this particular draft was discarded was Tocqueville's decision to gather in all the "intellectual effects" and give them another name—Cartesianism—and to treat only the isolation of hearts under the category of individualism. This was a major part of his contribution to the definition of the term: it is not an idea; it is an inner feeling, yet one that bears a family resemblance to ideas because of its calculating demeanor.

In his passion for France, Tocqueville now draws us back to America. "Individualism is more pronounced at the end of a democratic revolution than at any other time," he writes, clearly referring to France (508). But "the Americans have this great advantage, that they attained democracy without the sufferings of a democratic revolution and that they were born equal instead of becoming so" (509).

For most of the rest of part 2, Tocqueville discusses the ways the Americans blunt that isolation of heart and mind that he had identified in his "Rubish" as the price of individualism. It is this reattachment of Tocqueville to his empirical moorings, I believe, that makes part 2 superior to part 1. Here he discusses concretely the specific institutions and customs by which, knowingly or not, Americans deflect the isolation.

The structure of the rest of part 2 proves the point. From chapter 4 to chapter 14, Tocqueville's subject is isolation in America and especially Americans' unique efforts to "combat individualism" (525). Chapter 14 concerns "the taste for physical pleasures." After that descent into carnality, Tocqueville abruptly ascends to the heavens. In chapter 15, he explains how religion restrains desire; from this he derives lessons, in 16 and 17; and then, in three striking chapters, turns from pleasure to work, showing how work, as much as pleasure, isolates people from one another. But, as he will explain, it is pleasure, far more than work, that must be feared in a democracy.

The problem of isolation is fundamentally a political one. It clears a path for despotism and then guarantees its continuity. When citizens sequester themselves, each in his own tiny realm of sensation and thought, no one deliberates about the public good. Despots love and need this kind of self-regarding public apathy. Moreover, because "vices originating in despotism are precisely those favored by equality," the "peculiar need" of democratic times is a need for a counterbalancing freedom (509–10). But Americans have found the solution to this problem. They "have used liberty to combat the individualism born of equality," Tocqueville asserts, "and they have won" (511).

They have won because individualism's centrifugal tendencies are offset by the proliferation of free, locally based institutions, both governmental and nongovernmental. The governmental ("political") ones he had discussed in volume 1; now he explains how numerous private groups assemble to bring about projects for the public benefit. "Americans combine to give fêtes, found seminaries, build churches, distribute books, and send missionaries to the antipodes." Whenever a new enterprise is begun, "where in France you would find the government or in England some territorial magnate, in the United States you are sure to find an association" (513). Therefore, "nothing, in my view, more deserves attention than the intellectual and moral associations in America" (517). The prominence of these "intellectual and moral" organizations in Tocqueville's book reveals once again how vital he considered the proper kind of "ideas and feelings" to be for a society that desires to remain free as equality spreads.

In the first volume (part 2, chapters 3 and 4), Tocqueville described the importance of political associations. In this second volume, on civil society, he emphasizes how political interests "spread a general habit and taste for association" in civil life, as well (521).

Next to the chapter on individualism, the most famous portion of volume 2 is probably chapter 8 of part 2, in which Tocqueville introduces one of the three concepts for which he is best known: "self-interest properly understood." (The other two are "tyranny of the majority" and "individualism" itself.) Because American individualism straddles the boundary of ideas and sentiments, the formula can be seen as a further refinement of that "calm and considered feeling." "Properly understood," self-interest leads Americans to recognize the benefits to themselves as calculating individuals of concerted public action through associations. The salient comparison for American individualism, of course, is with France and its egoism. In America, egoism is "enlightened," Tocqueville observes; "here it is not." The distinction is urgent, because as democracy spreads "private interest will more than ever become the driving force behind all behavior" (527). France must therefore learn to leaven its heedless egoism with sound judgment.

At a deeper level, Tocqueville is saying still more: with the passing of the aristocratic age morality itself is being transformed. Aristocratic morality had been based on a peculiar conception of virtue, according to which "one should do good without self-interest, as God himself does. . . . Only in secret did [men] study its utility" (525). But in the new age of equality, utility is uppermost in citizens' minds and hearts, and the new challenge is not to combat it, a useless task in any case, but to harness it, to educate it. "The age of blind sacrifice and instinctive virtues"—the aristocratic age—"is already long past," he writes (528), once more associating France with blindness and instinct. The new era, however, demands not instinct, but calculation. The essential political problem for France might therefore be expressed as follows: her people have passed from the aristocratic to the democratic era without having divested themselves of the blind instincts and passions appropriate to the vanished past. Conversely, and by way of example, the Americans, whose experience of equality originates from their very point of departure as a people, have learned to tether their desires to a realistic understanding of the interplay between private acquisitiveness and public agitation.

Yet if Tocqueville was almost Marxian in his theorizing about the social bases of morality, he was virtually Weberian in his recognition of the connections between such morality and economic activity. Tocqueville still maintained at the time of the 1840 volume an intellectually intimate friendship with John Stuart Mill, who besides being the Anglo-American world's leading philosopher of liberty was also a pioneer of the new science of political economy—the field we now designate as economics. He had also struck up a friendship with the English economist Nassau Senior, the chief theorist of the abstinence theory of capital, the notion that capital originates in abstention from immediate gratification and that such abstinence, however incidentally, justifies profits as a return to capital in a market system.

Whether as a result of the contacts with Mill and Senior, or because it fit his own sense of a democratic state founded without revolution, Tocqueville saw how certain constraints on desire were fundamental to the developing capitalist economy. In America, he observes, "love of comfort has become the dominant national taste. The main current of human passions running in that direction sweeps everything along with it." But "the passion for physical pleasures produces in democracies effects very different from those it occasions in aristocratic societies" (532). Specifically, this "universal passion" is also "a restrained one" in such societies. In making this crucial observation, Tocqueville also pointed to a central difference between capitalism and other economic regimes, namely that in capitalism, wealth is dedicated to the accumulation of wealth as capital and not simply amassed for aggrandizement or mere pleasure. "There is no question of building vast palaces . . . or sucking the world dry to satisfy one man's greed. It is more a question of adding a few acres to one's fields." Such "petty aims . . . sometimes come between the soul and God," Tocqueville knew, but it also means that "in democracies the taste for physical pleasures takes special forms which are not opposed by their nature to good order" (533).

This is not to say that the Americans' dogged repression of their instincts, their tendency to bank the fires of egoism by coldly calculating their self-interest, is not balanced by any celestial concerns; it is, and those concerns often come in the rather alarming shape of "enthusiastic forms of spirituality." Tocqueville observes, with a somewhat patronizing tone that masks his lack of a deeper understanding, the ascendancy of "strange sects," a sort of "religious madness" and an "enthusiastic, almost fierce spirituality"—in short, he notes the "Second Great Awakening" that swept the United States at approximately the time of his visit (534). But he understands it only in terms of the categories he had established in earlier chapters. It was utterly predictable, he thought, that "in a society thinking about nothing but the world a few individuals should want to look at nothing but heaven" (535).

For the rest of part 2, the Americans may be observed hovering halfway between debasement and exaltation as Tocqueville tries to show how the earthward pull of their materialism encounters resistance from uplifting spiritual and even political forces. The consequence is a kind of dynamic moderation that pointedly contrasts with the extreme pitching and reeling of the French ship of state. France's instinctive egoism on the one hand, and, on the other, its propensity for airy speculation, produce not the healthy tension of an Aristotelian mean, but the violence of repeated shifts to one or the other extreme. The contrast reveals once again that quality of American restlessness and agitation, rather than chaos, that Tocqueville continually puts forward as a paradigm of a healthy polity.

There is an American passion, to be sure: the passion for riches. "It is odd," Tocqueville writes, "to watch with what feverish ardor the Americans pursue prosperity and how they are ever tormented by the shadowy suspicion that they may not have chosen the shortest route to get it" (537). But as was the case with respect to intellectual proclivities, so also in the realm of sentiments do American conditions modify the extreme. There, the craving for pleasure is restrained by three factors: a "love of freedom," "attention to public affairs," and religion, "the most precious heritage from aristocratic times" (540, 544).

Note that these same factors, freedom, public participation, and religion, do double duty. They are the same ones that act to curb the excess that occurs in the intellectual life of a democratic age—namely, that tendency of the mind to float away on a balloon of gassy generalizations, unconstrained by empirical concerns. In chapters 4 and 5 of part 1 espe-

cially, Tocqueville observed the palliative effects of those factors. He concluded chapter 4 with a cogent summary: "Democratic institutions
which make each citizen take a practical part in government moderate
the excessive taste for general political theories which is prompted by
equality" (442); while in chapter 5 he had shown how religion "imposes
on each man some obligations toward mankind . . . and so draws him
away, from time to time, from thinking about himself" (444–45). Now
he extends his analysis to show how religion and public participation
curb the dominant "sentiment" of democracy, as well—the potentially
unlimited desire for wealth and "physical pleasures."

That craving, Tocqueville knew, is a brutish one. Throughout
Democracy in America, but especially here in part 2, he discloses, sometimes, I think, unconsciously, a fear of regression to a lower stage of
social development. The concern about despotism and slavery is, in part,
an anxiety about social arrangements associated with those previous
stages. It is precisely France's flirtations with despotism that make her
own advancement an open question. The specific danger for democracies, where men and women are preoccupied by the satisfaction of their
desires as consumers, is that their political concerns will narrow to a
mere desire for public order. That way lies the road to despotism: "A
nation which asks nothing from the government beyond the maintenance of order is already a slave in the bottom of its heart" (540). While
the Americans have eluded that particular danger for now, it will certainly reemerge, for the taste for physical pleasures is by nature ever
expanding. In pursuing satisfaction, people may deprive themselves of
"the art of producing" and end up "like animals" (547).

Part 2 ends with three chapters on labor. The last of these, on "How
an Aristocracy May Be Created by Industry," is among the most
prophetic in a book that won its author an almost unrivaled reputation
for prescience. Tocqueville describes the phenomenon Marx would soon
call *alienation*, the process by which the product of the worker's art and
labor, and ultimately his very identity, come to be experienced as something outside of himself. As the division of labor produces ever finer gra-
dations in the production process and the skill of the worker becomes
ever more specialized and restricted in scope, his "general faculty of
applying his mind" atrophies. "The man is degraded as the workman
improves," and in the end "he no longer belongs to himself" (555).

What is most striking about this chapter, however—at least from the
perspective from which Tocqueville's work has been expounded in this
book—is the way Tocqueville shows how this "sentiment" of alienation[11]

occurs in a social setting that bears a direct analogy to the old aristocratic milieu. But this is a new kind of aristocracy, "not at all like those that have preceded it," because unlike its feudal predecessor, "it is an exception, a monstrosity, within the general social condition" (557). Thus, industrialism provides a fissure through which a new kind of tyranny might filter into the democratic social order still in the making. "In any event, the friends of democracy should keep their eyes anxiously fixed in that direction. For if ever again permanent inequality of conditions and aristocracy make their way into the world, it will have been by that door that they entered" (558).

Thus ends the first half of the second volume. Parts 1 and 2, while treating the intellect and the emotions as two distinct spheres of human interiority (or so it was thought in the nineteenth century), are complementary in philosophical and rhetorical as well as psychological terms. As may be clear by this stage of the walking tour, Tocqueville saw Cartesianism and individualism as counterparts. Cartesianism is to the head as individualism is to the heart. The first is a form of solitude and exaggerated independence in the realm of ideas, the second of detachment and isolation of the feelings. Likewise, the two concepts carry their own extreme dangers. For Cartesianism, the intellectual sin or extreme is the "passion for conceptions," a "blind faith in the virtue and absolute truth of any theory" (441). The extreme of individualism, the sin of the heart, is egoism.

There is another important affinity between the two parts. They are situated on a vertical axis. At the zenith is the intellectual extreme—an excess of speculative generalization, a love of "exalted" general theories unconstrained by any inconvenient reference to the untidy realities of earthbound human societies. This is the subject of part 1. At the nadir lies the "base" sentiment of egoism, "a vice as old as the world" that "springs from blind instinct" (507, 506). This extreme in the domain of feeling is brought into relief in part 2. In both areas, Tocqueville seeks to show, the Americans have avoided the excesses. They use their freedom and their religion, first, to combat the tendency to embrace the most abstract theoretical propositions, and second, to uplift their gaze from the delights of consumption and physical pleasure. But France has not developed the institutions and customs necessary to contend with the new regime of equality; in that lacerated country "democracy has been abandoned to its wild instincts" (13).

The verticality of parts 1 and 2 will be displaced by an outward, expansive flow in parts 3 and 4. And where the first two parts were psy-

chological, dealing with the effects of equality on the soul, the remainder
will be sociological and political, concerned with the effects this kind of
a citizenry has on mores and on what recent political philosophers call
"political culture," that is, the whole context of thought and practice in
which political institutions function.[12]

What Is Essential in Man

Part 3 is concerned with "mores properly so called" (559). But why
did Tocqueville add the qualifier? He was a writer of the greatest precision and lucidity who almost never let slip a shoddy phrase or formulation. Why, then, "properly so called"? Was there some flaw or defect in
the unvarnished term *mores*? In fact, there was, and Tocqueville ought to
have reminded his readers what the problem was, as he had in volume 1,
for the difficulty persists in some sociological circles even today. It is the
tendency to think of mores solely as "habits of the heart," that is, as
behavior shaped by feelings separate from any intellectual content.

In fact, Tocqueville had done much to clarify the full meaning of the
term *moeurs* in the first volume. By *moeurs*, he wrote then, he referred not
only to "the habits of the heart, but also to the different notions possessed by men, the various opinions current among them, and the sum
of ideas that shape mental habits. So I use the word to cover the whole
moral and intellectual state of a people" (287).

Thus the importance of the qualifier: the behavior patterns he is
about to analyze spring from the twin sources he has so carefully expli-
cated in the preceding two parts—both the ideas and the feelings that
democracy prompts in citizens' minds and hearts. The first two parts of
the volume describe a new, modern personality type. The last two show
what kind of behavior this democratic personality displays.

Such behavior encompasses more than "customs," important as these
are, for the word *mores* bears in its etymology traces of its origins in the
discourse of morality. People's behavior entails and bespeaks at least to
some extent consciously chosen values; thus *mores* casts a wider net than
the term *customs*, which denotes any behavior that is collective, habitual,
and patterned. Mores have an ethical significance.

Finally, it is vital at this point to recall that, in the opening pages of
the first volume, Tocqueville had attributed the ascendancy of democracy to progress in the intellectual sphere. As he wrote in the "Author's
Introduction" about the earliest stirrings of equality: "The mind became
an element in success; knowledge became a tool of government and

intellect a social force" (10). This dimension of the mind—which is also an ethical dimension—is essential to understanding Tocqueville's conception of democratic mores. They must not be considered a matter of the heart alone.

Once again, a careful, intricate structure undergirds the argument of this as well as the other parts of volume 2. Its 26 chapters can be divided into six sections, each of which is between three and five chapters long, punctuated by two chapters that encompass themes previously presented:

Chapters 1–4: theory of mores in a democracy
Chapters 5–7: effects on economic life and contracts
Chapters 8–12: effects on women and the family
Chapter 13: withdrawal into small private circles
Chapters 14–16: effects on manners
Chapters 17–20: effects on the values of honor and ambition
Chapter 21: the question of revolution or docility
Chapters 22–26: armies and the contradictions of equality

Democratic mores, like the intellectual and emotional impulses from which they spring, display a few broad tendencies which, once identified, can be employed to predict social behavior. According to Tocqueville, the essential force driving conduct in democratic societies is that in them "people become more like one another" (565), as do social conditions.

This postulate of increasing homogeneity seems at first to be one of the most arguable in all of Tocqueville. For the moment he left the United States, historically speaking, the ethnically homogeneous society he had visited dissolved in a bath of immigration. From 1815 to 1830, the United States took in about 30,000 immigrants per year. But in the 1830s, 600,000 newcomers arrived; in the 1840s, 1.7 million; and after 1850, a deluge—more than 2.7 million.[13] German Jews and Irish Catholics now took their places alongside the Protestant "Anglo-Americans" in the democratic citizenry of the United States.

Tocqueville had dealt brilliantly with heterogeneity and otherness at the end of volume 1, in his report on "the three races." Each of them, red, black, and white, he had said then, "follows a separate destiny"—although we might well surmise, with Ralph Lerner, that "each has marked the other and has done so in a way that shows another hue of the American democrat."[14]

That chapter, however, as Tocqueville explicitly says, was about America but not about democracy. "There are other things in America besides an immense and complete democracy," he caustically remarks (316). In analyzing mores, however, Tocqueville was interested in precisely that which *is* democratic. The issue, then, revolves not around ethnicity but how the immigrants' social behavior was modified over time. Insofar as assimilation occurred, the Tocquevillian hypothesis, it can be argued, was experimentally confirmed.

Tocqueville then shows how the mores of democracy affect economic relations. For example, American mobility causes landlords to factor that restlessness into the terms of their leases, shortening their duration and raising the rent. And capitalists, who as Adam Smith noted never get together for more than a minute without colluding, are in a position to keep wages depressed because the workers in their multitude cannot combine with the ease of their bosses.

Of particular interest is a comparatively long chapter on masters and servants, which, despite enormous differences in the subject matter, temperaments, and objectives of their authors, invites comparison with Hegel's famous, nearly contemporary analysis of lordship and bondage in *Phenomenology of Spirit*.[15] Tocqueville insightfully characterizes servants' behavior in aristocracies as "a sort of servile honor." Not just another clever Tocquevillian oxymoron, this phrase is also an observation on the self-identification of servants with their masters. Yet servants "do not understand fame, virtue, honesty, and honor in the same way as their masters. . . . In aristocracies servants are a class apart, which changes no more than that of the masters. . . . There are two societies imposed one on top of the other, always distinct, but with analogous principles" (573). The extreme of aristocratic servitude, the lackey, serves to represent "the ultimate designation of human meanness" (574). At the same time, "the master comes to think of his servants as an inferior and secondary part of himself" (575).

Tocqueville is much less sensitive than Hegel to the full reciprocity of self-awareness, to the fact that "the lord [as well as the lackey] achieves his recognition through another consciousness."[16] In fact, the major contrast between Hegel and Tocqueville revolves on just this point. Hegel's insight was that both lord and servant achieve self-consciousness through their primitive encounter; while Tocqueville posits as an "extreme case" the servant drained of his individuality. Bereft of "his sense of self-interest[,] he becomes detached from it; he deserts himself, as it were, or rather he transports the whole of himself into his master's character." But he recognized their inextricable interconnectedness: "On the one side, obscurity, poverty, and obedience forever; on the other, fame, wealth, and power to command forever. Their lots are always different and always close, and the link between them is as lasting as life itself" (575).

Still more to the point, perhaps, is the recognition by both thinkers of the primal nature of this relation: for Hegel, to be sure, it is an interior, psychological primacy; for Tocqueville, a historical and social one. For as Tocqueville goes on to say, with the coming of a new social order—*démocratie*—the social type of the detached servant disappears, as does the "servile honor" that validated it. This issue is fundamental to democracy and to the future. In the United States, the social types of the trusted retainer and the lackey are "lost without trace." Master and servant have been replaced by autonomous agents operating through free contract. A servant is just an employee. The master-servant relationship has been transformed into a contract stipulation, outside of which the contracting parties are simply "two citizens, two men" (576). Understanding this contrast is central to the task of projecting the shape of a future society.

Hence this chapter on masters and servants functions in a manner parallel to the one on science in the section on ideas. As with the science chapter, it comes after a section in which a theory had been laid out, it functions as the first practical application of that theory, and it serves as a paradigm of what is to come. The new, contractual, independent relationship of masters and servants is actually a model of democratic mores.

So we learn that "public opinion . . . creates a sort of fancied equality between them, in spite of the actual inequality of their lives" (577). The two parties develop no emotional ties; they look upon command and obedience as provisions in a contract rather than duties sanctioned by timeless custom or the divine order; and their interaction is laced with neither pride nor humility.

This prototype informs all the other examples of democratic mores. But to Tocqueville, it is a prototype not merely of democracy but of all humanity. The onward march of homogeneity, the gradual disappearance of variety that accompanies the weakening of antiquated class rigidities, means that democratic mores are "getting closer to what is essential in man" (615). Because aristocracy is not natural, democracy is closer to man's true nature. As Marvin Zetterbaum noted, "The democratic revolution, accompanied as it is by the disappearance of aristocratic forms, is thus the agency by which man's nature is revealed. Inquiry into the nature of democratic man is thus inquiry into the nature of man per se." Consequently, "the democratic condition does not so much alter man's nature as bring it to the fore, and allow and encourage it to express itself."[17]

But it must be noted, as Zetterbaum does not, that democracy's naturalness has a distinctive trait that first surfaced in volume 1. Democracy is indeed the natural condition of humanity, but humanity at a particular moment in the drama of its cultural evolution. It is not a form of regression to a precivilized state. Far from belonging "to the earliest ages of the world," Tocqueville had written in volume 1, democracy "could only have come last" (208). Tocqueville's view of human nature, then, is a dynamic one. He views democracy as the natural condition not of all humanity for all time, but of men and women in the modern world.

Nevertheless, there is a danger that, when the mystifying artifice of aristocracy is torn away, it will be replaced not with the healthful, stabilizing artifice of democracy—the associations, parties, newspapers, and other appurtenances of a vital public life—but by barbarism. There is a perilous moment in the transition between aristocracy and democracy, especially for "the European peoples," when "by becoming democratic they run the risk of falling back into a sort of barbarism," he had written in an early draft of volume 2.[18] Americans, not having had experience with the aristocratic age, are spared such an inclination to anarchy, that temptation to tear away the aristocratic forms and proclaim the resultant natural order both necessary and sufficient to human happiness.

There are two areas in which Tocqueville probed the effects of democratic mores and reached conclusions that still seem remarkably fresh. One was a feminine, the other a masculine, sphere. His analysis of gender roles—of women in relation to marriage, courtship, education, and the family, and of men's relation to the virtues of honor and ambition—revealed the limitations of democratic mores.

Chapters 9 through 12, on women, demand special attention, for two reasons: first, because they reveal the tensions between social equality and the nineteenth-century "cult of domesticity," and second, because this part of *Democracy in America* is about mores and, Tocqueville says, "it is woman who shapes these mores" (590). While aristocracies are shaped by the principles and ideology of patriarchy ("In aristocracies society is, in all truth, only concerned with the father" [586]), democratic ages, gentler in tone and manners, are more under the sway of women. Indeed, women in the United States occupy a status of near equality with men. It is a starkly limited equality, however, and one highly dependent on lip service. (Soon, moreover, women's cul-

tural authority would, in Ann Douglas's term, be "disestablished.")[19]
Tocqueville seems to have made his observations of women's status and
role at a high-water mark.

To describe women's position, Tocqueville selected a metaphor that is
at once arresting in its aptness and somewhat chilling in its detachment.
"The Americans," he says, "have applied to the sexes the great principle
of political economy which now dominates industry." That principle, of
course, is the division of labor. The Americans do advance the equality of
women, but do so by exalting their position within a rigorously restricted sphere, the family. Indeed, precisely insofar as woman's status is
raised, to just that extent is her entrapment in her own domain made
more inflexible. "In America, more than anywhere else in the world, care
has been taken constantly to trace clearly distinct spheres of action for
the two sexes" (601). Here in the strict separation of these "clear" and
"distinct" spheres—terms Tocqueville cannot have chosen carelessly—
American Cartesianism resurfaces with a vengeance. It is not surprising
to find Tocqueville's pages on women quoted enthusiastically and at
great length, just one year after their publication, in Catharine Beecher's
best-selling program for elevating women's condition while restricting
the compass of their activities, *A Treatise on Domestic Economy*.[20]

Yet restrictions on women are ubiquitous, not confined to the United
States. Tocqueville frankly praises the progress or advancement of
women within their spheres and sees it as characteristic of democratic
mores. "While [the Americans] have allowed the social inferiority of
woman to continue, they have done everything to raise her morally and
intellectually to the level of man." And he attributed "the extraordinary
prosperity and growing power of this nation . . . to the superiority of
their women" (603). The context of this famous encomium ought to be
remembered, however: it is democratic mores that permit such prosperity and power, and women are their source.

The discussion of the values of the masculine sphere, honor and ambition, follows a course of argument that the analysis of masters and servants had laid out. Honor is the name given to the rules of behavior for
particular segments of society. As society loses its distinctive castes, however, and as social conditions continue to drive men into "trade and
industry," honor becomes, as it were, domesticated. "Those quiet virtues
which tend to regularity in the body social and which favor trade"
become the objects of homage and respect (621). Thus, "that which our
ancestors called, par excellence, honor was really only one of its forms.

They gave the name of a genus to what was in fact only a species" (623). Likewise, "lofty ambitions" have become scarce, and, when met with, seem to possess "a violent and revolutionary character" (631). This near-perfect and ever-advancing sameness is like all the phenomena under examination laden with both dangers and opportunities. Tocqueville's two greatest fears were revolution and apathy. The new social conditions contained the potential for either disaster. Because "trade is the natural enemy of all violent passions" (637), and "men's main opinions become alike as the conditions of their lives become alike" (641), the chances for revolutionary upheaval would diminish. But even more to be feared was a political and social lassitude springing from those same conditions. "What frightens me most," he says unequivocally, "is the danger that . . . human passions may grow gentler and at the same time baser, with the result that the progress of the body social may become daily quieter and less aspiring" (632). A few pages later, the frightening image of the vortex appears: "I fear that the mind may keep folding itself up in a narrower compass forever" (645). Of the two hazards, then—revolution and lassitude—the latter is by far the greater. For, as Tocqueville shows in the solemn final section of his book, it can spawn both anarchy and despotism.

So deep is Tocqueville's sense of the perils of apathy, in fact, that it even leads him to entertain thoughts of the advantages of war. "I do not wish to speak ill of war," he writes; "war almost always widens a nation's mental horizons and raises its heart." Such "widening" and "raising" of minds and hearts is, we recall, essential in offsetting the downward pull of materialism. In 1840, however, Tocqueville was not willing to advocate armed conflict as a positive remedy for apathy. This great liberal perceived the contradiction he was heading toward, and in typical fashion registered the converse of his first position: "War has great advantages, but we must not flatter ourselves that it can lessen the danger I have just pointed out. It only puts the danger off, to come back in more terrible form when war is over" (649). In later years, when he had fewer reservations about the therapeutic benefits of war for a lethargic population, he would have done well to heed his own warning.

Tocqueville's ruminations on war are part of the conclusion to part 3. His attention at the end of this section on mores is on armies and, more generally, the problem of military ambition—an aristocratic attribute— in a society so utterly out of step with such aspirations. The army, in fact, is like industry in being a contradiction of democratic society. The mili-

tary life offers scope for the ambition of aspiring young men, but democratic ages call for "those quiet virtues . . . which favor trade." The contradiction thus arises of "democratic peoples [wanting] peace but democratic armies war" (645). But Tocqueville followed the logic of democracy further and drew a picture of a democratic society at war that reflected 1865, 1918, even 1944: "War . . . in the end becomes itself the one great industry, and every eager and ambitious desire sprung from equality is focused on it" (657).

He perceived, too, that democracies—that is, societies whose mores are fashioned by equality—face a unique vulnerability. Without freedom, they are naked to their enemies. "It is only passion for freedom, habitually enjoyed, which can do more than hold its own against a habitual absorption in well-being. I can imagine nothing better prepared, in case of defeat, for conquest than a democratic people without free institutions" (663).

An Immense, Protective Power

"I have vainly searched for a word. . . . Old words . . . do not fit. The thing is new . . . I cannot find a word for it" (691).

This stammer, this blank at the very heart of Tocqueville's book, is in part, as Jean-Claude Lamberti contends, a failure of performance. Lamberti is persuasive in maintaining that at the very end of his work Tocqueville stumbled. In putting forward a political program in part 4 of volume 2, "some aspects of his thought are, through his own fault, fairly obscure." And, as a result, "the published text is but a pale and confused version of Tocqueville's thinking."[21]

But an additional reason for this anomalous lapse of eloquence lies where Tocqueville said it did, in the novelty of the object under investigation, and in the resulting lack of a new term to name the new thing. So, instead of naming it right away, Tocqueville reveals a vision that floats before his eyes:

> I see an innumerable multitude of men, alike and equal, constantly circling around in pursuit of the petty and banal pleasures with which they glut their souls. Each one of them, withdrawn into himself, is almost unaware of the fate of the rest. Mankind, for him, consists in his children and his personal friends. As for the rest of his fellow citizens, they are near enough, but he does not notice them. He touches them but feels nothing. He exists in and for himself, and though he still may have a family, one can at least say that he has not got a fatherland.

Over this kind of men stands an immense, protective power which is alone responsible for securing their enjoyment and watching over their fate. That power is absolute, thoughtful of detail, orderly, provident, and gentle. (691–92)

There was an obvious term to hand for the chilling spectacle Tocqueville displays: it is a form of despotism. But Tocqueville was reluctant to use that word. Like individualism or tyranny of the majority, the phenomenon he was describing was something without precedent, something even Montesquieu had not foreseen, something *modern*, the full comprehension of which demanded the use of terms uncontaminated by their association with archaic forms of domination. In the end, however, he was forced by the pressure of meaning in the concept and by the absence of an adequate discourse to describe it, into forging another oxymoron. And so he gave it the name "democratic despotism." I believe that the entire development of Tocqueville's thought about this key political formation of the modern world leads to the conclusion that both his reluctance to use despotism, and the resultant frustrating search for a new term, spring from the connotation that links despotism with older categories of servitude. "The type of oppression which threatens democracies is different from anything there has ever been in the world before. . . . Such old words as 'despotism' and 'tyranny' do not fit" (691). Thus, although this modern kind of subjection directed at "our contemporaries" (693) would have to be understood as analogous to previous kinds of subjection, it is different in a fundamental way.[22]

To comprehend its meaning for Tocqueville, as for ourselves, we might turn again to the structure of the book. Tocqueville explicitly connects democratic despotism with the feelings, thoughts, and resultant mores of democratic citizens. The danger that is then presented in part 4 can be summarized as follows: the free instincts of democratic peoples are in conflict with their mores. The outcome of that conflict will be determined by the interaction of a number of independent variables. But only one of those variables, and perhaps not the most significant one, involves free human choice.

Reverting to the arrangement he first employed in part 2, Tocqueville explains how democracy spawns characteristic instincts, or unreflective inclinations, in its citizens. He uses such terms as "natural bias," "basic instincts," and "instinctive inclination" to indicate how people in a democracy are predisposed toward free institutions (667–68). Then he shows how the "ideas," "feelings," and resultant "habits" of democracies incline them toward centralization and the concentration of political power. Thus, democracies have split personalities: a subliminal desire for liberty cohabits in the same breast with conscious ideas and emotions that paradoxically undermine that very desire.

To begin with the ideas: certain concepts, especially that of powers that act as intermediaries between the people and the government, arose quite naturally in aristocracies. But equality gives rise to the opposite notion, namely that of "a single central power directing all citizens" (668).

Moreover, while "men readily conceive" this idea, "both their habits and their feelings" incline them to advance it. There is, first of all, that "habit" of isolation, that egoism or individualism, which causes them to want to leave the collective interests of the society to others to look after while they themselves pursue the gratifications of consumption; and as there is but one institution to which those interests are entrusted—the state—the tendency is to hand over public affairs to it alone.

Then there is the overwhelming "feeling" of democratic society, "the increasing love of well-being," which leads to a desiccation of all political passions save the passion for order (671). This, too, feeds the state's power. Thus, "two different paths," both thought and feeling, "mind and heart," lead toward "one sole uniform and strong government" (673).

Tocqueville's explicit contention at the end of his book, then, is that thoughts, feelings, and mores in democracies all tend toward a new kind of despotism and that they are counteracted chiefly by a dimly understood instinct for free institutions. His task, only slightly less explicit, is to elevate the awareness of the instinct for liberty to the level of conscious thought; or, to change the metaphor, to illuminate that dim desire with his book and to show how the "instinctive inclination toward political freedom" nurtured by equality is "the antidote for the ill which [equality] has produced" (668).

Whether people will be led toward centralization or away from it will largely be determined by accidents, by the "particular circumstances" of each case. But the key "accidental cause" is "the way in which that equality was established" (675). If people have known freedom before equality, the habits of that freedom will tend to persevere. If, on the other hand, the equality develops among people for whom freedom is a novelty, "all powers seem spontaneously to rush to the center" (674). Of course, the English settlers we find at the American point of departure knew freedom first, while in Europe equality developed before the people could experience liberty. "Thus, in America it is freedom that is old, and equality is comparatively new. The opposite obtains in Europe" (675). There "the citizens are perpetually falling under the control of the public administration." Once more, the essential distinction is whether the equality originates from revolution, and Tocqueville "venture[s] once more to repeat what I have already said or implied in several places in this book. One must be careful not to confuse the fact of equality with the revolution which succeeds in introducing it into the state of society and into the laws" (688).

If the habits, inclinations, feelings, ideas, mores, history, and all the variables Tocqueville has identified, plus the vitally important imponderable of free human decision, fail to protect liberty, the alternative is a new kind of oppression, which he finally labels "democratic despotism" (692). He focused on the softness of this despotism, the degree to which it "leads [men and women] to give up using their free will . . . and enervates their souls" (694).

With another prophetic warning, Tocqueville ended his book and took up a new career to thwart the perils he dreaded. Elected to the Chamber in 1839, he barely had time to finish volume 2 before taking up his duties in Paris.

One cannot say, he wrote in his final footnote, whether anarchy or despotism presents the greater danger. What is clear is that both "spring from one and the same cause, that is the *general apathy*, the fruit of individualism. . . . We should therefore direct our efforts, not against anarchy or despotism, but against the apathy which could engender one or the other almost indifferently" (735–36 n. BB).

The themes that gripped the brilliant, earnest, young aristocrat astonished at the great moving tableau of democracy in the 1830s would recur throughout the rest of his life, taking different forms, analyzed from different perspectives with different methodologies, but always, in some fundamental sense, the same: the fear of lethargy, the need for action—at times, it seemed, any action—to rouse the spirit and bring men and women out of the ever-narrowing compass of their own isolated selves.

Chapter Four
Commerce, Civilization, and Outsiders

France labors to create civilized societies, not hordes of savages.

—TOCQUEVILLE, "REPORT ON THE ABOLITION OF SLAVERY" (1839)

This chapter is about the place of some of the nineteenth century's marginalized groups—paupers, Native Americans, criminals, and former slaves—in Tocqueville's work. It presents an argument derived from my investigation of an ill-understood corner of Tocqueville's intellectual milieu: the nineteenth century's still-developing belief in the evolution of human culture through a series of stages that came to bear the labels savage, barbarian, and civilized.

The ever-expanding web of market relations in the early nineteenth century produced myriad paradoxical effects, among which were the simultaneous increase of political equality and social inequality. Tocqueville understood this paradox as clearly as anyone. But, at a deeper level, he also perceived the fact that whole great collectivities of persons were in danger of being left behind by the trajectory of history. He tended to view this issue through the lens of the aforementioned conception of cultural evolution. It not only helped account for the origins of the problem, but it also pointed to possible courses of action for its solution.

Tocqueville believed that it was in part through their participation in market society, and especially in labor markets, that the semibarbarous outsider groups could be folded into the great course of historical development. To be uncivilized was to be chaotic, unordered, transient, unsettled. Markets provided discipline, not only over inward desire, but also over external disorder. Persons unfamiliar with the workings of the market—former slaves, for instance—needed to receive guidance and assistance in understanding the importance of entering new networks of market relations; if such guidance were not sufficient, a measure of coercion would be called for. In his 1839 report to the Chamber of Deputies on the abolition of slavery in the French colonies, for example, Tocqueville wrote that, while the state ought to "first show [the freed-

81

man} and then, if necessary, pressure him into the arduous and manly habits of liberty," it may become necessary to "impose those conditions . . . and compel their submission" ("Report," 117, 133). Furthermore, those "conditions" bringing about the desired "manly habits of liberty" were spelled out in an 1843 article Tocqueville wrote for *Le Siècle*, a newspaper of the Bourbon opposition to Louis Philippe. Freed colonial blacks must be prevented from establishing themselves as independent peasants, he wrote, and made instead to enter the labor market, working for wages on their former masters' estates.[1]

Yet Tocqueville also believed that the civilizing powers of markets faced distinct limits, since there were paradoxically barbarous consequences of participation in a society based on such relations. Commercial societies, he thought, rather rapidly attained the limits of their civilizing ability and shortly began to induce a lethargy or torpor, an enervation of public life, which in turn led to the same sort of disorder and despotism that characterized barbarism. Commerce and civilization thus coexisted in a state of tension, the former being essential to the development of civilization, but, in excess, fatal to it. Thus, while market society could provide, through labor and abstinence, a point of entry to civilized life for those left behind, it also constituted a point of exit for people who became too enamored of the charms of consumption.

Indians

Embarking for New Orleans from Memphis on a Mississippi steamboat on Christmas Day in 1831, Tocqueville and Beaumont found themselves accidental witnesses to a sobering and unforgettable spectacle. A group of exiled Choctaws, forced off their lands by President Andrew Jackson's removal policy, filed onto the steamboat on the last portion of their tragic journey, their "Trail of Tears," heading for a destination in remote, unknown Arkansas. Tocqueville found in the scene "an air of ruin and destruction, something that savored of a farewell that was final." He and Beaumont knew, as he wrote to his mother, that they were witnessing not merely the "expulsion," but "the dissolution of one of the most celebrated and most ancient American nations."[2]

This was not, however, the young traveler's first encounter with America's aboriginal "savages." In Buffalo the summer before, they had been both fascinated and repelled by a band of Iroquois. Expecting to find aesthetic specimens out of Cooper and Chateaubriand, "savages in whose features nature had left the trace of . . . those proud virtues born of liberty," and "men whose bodies had been developed by hunting and war, and who would lose nothing by being seen nude" (*J*, 351–52), they discovered instead a pathetic collection of emaciated figures. Far from being athletic and "developed," he wrote, "the Indians . . . were small in stature; their limbs . . . thin and far from muscular; their skin, instead of being of the copper-red colour that is generally supposed, was dark bronze, . . . very like that of mulattoes." Their faces bore "vicious" expressions; indeed "their physiognomy told of that profound degradation that can only be reached by a long abuse of the benefits of civilization." Significantly, and logically, Tocqueville then associated this savage remnant with paupers. "One would have said they were men from the lowest mob of our great European cities. And yet they are still savages." These people had developed as a sort of cultural monstrosity: a bit of degraded civilization had been grafted prematurely onto a savage stock, resulting in a hybrid that reveals neither the grandeur of civilization nor the dignity that results from a life of liberty, hunting, and war. "Mixed up with the vices they got from us was something barbarous and uncivilised that made them a hundred times more repulsive still" (*J*, 352).

Characteristically, Tocqueville was quick to add that such a sight was not to be taken as a portrait of all Native Americans; that, indeed, it was an aberration. How much so would be made clear in the following days.

A few weeks later, while proceeding through the Michigan wilderness on their excursion to Saginaw, Tocqueville and Beaumont were startled to observe an Indian who had apparently been following them for some time. Tocqueville portrayed this man in terms very different from that of the Iroquois of Buffalo. "He was a man of about thirty, large and wonderfully well proportioned as they almost all are." In contrast to the Iroquois, who, although they wore European clothes, "did not use them in the same way as we do," this man, a Chippewa, "was dressed in a sort of very short blue blouse. He wore red mittas—they are a sort of trousers that only come to the thighs—and his feet were clad in moccasins" (*J*, 373). This handsome and friendly "savage" followed them for some miles until he came to the land of his own people.

A key to understanding the contrasts in these descriptions can be discovered in Tocqueville's interview with Sam Houston, just a day after the Choctaws disembarked from the steamboat in Arkansas. The former governor of Tennessee, soon to be the president of Texas, married at that time to a Creek and himself a chief, gave Tocqueville an analysis of the "degrees of civilization" among the native Americans.

> At the head of all come the *Cherokees*. The *Cherokees* live entirely by cultivating the soil. They are the only Indian tribe that has a written language.
>
> After the *Cherokees* come the *Creeks*. The *Creeks* subsist partly from hunting and partly from cultivating some land. They have some definite penal laws and a form of government.
>
> Next I place the *Chickasaws* and the *Choctaws*. One cannot yet say that they have begun to get civilized, but they have begun to lose many of the traits of their savage nature.
>
> The *Osages* come last of all; they live in continually moving hordes, are almost naked, hardly use firearms at all, and know no Europeans except the fur traders. (*J*, 256)

What we might designate "Sam Houston's Taxonomy" is a good shorthand description of a means of comprehending non-European peoples that has its origins in eighteenth-century Scotland, with forerunners as early as the seventeenth century in France.[3] According to this tradition, peoples move through distinct stages called savagery, barbarism, and civilization, with each stage being characterized by its own distinct material and spiritual attributes.

In the Scottish tradition, Adam Smith and John Millar had described a four-stage process. Each stage was based on means of subsistence, although the theory was far from being purely materialist. Indeed certain ideas, like the idea of property, were held to have exerted an immense and independent influence in man's social development. The four stages were labeled the hunting-gathering, pastoral, agricultural, and commercial. For a while, the three- and four-stage theories coexisted, but the three-level scheme ultimately prevailed, as the second and third stages—pastoral and agricultural—were collapsed into a single phase encompassed by the term barbarism.

By examining the endpoint of the development of the three-phase structure, we can perceive more clearly the template Tocqueville used for understanding the Native Americans. That endpoint came in the work of the remarkable Lewis Henry Morgan of Rochester, New York, a lawyer, amateur ethnologist, and an important scholar of the Iroquois Federation, whose major work, *Ancient Society* (1877), although it now sits unused in obscure corners of dusty libraries, was in its day considered a major contribution to the human sciences. Karl Marx, for one important example, considered *Ancient Society* to have been the definitive study of early man. In fact, Marx planned to write a book about Morgan's principles. He filled a notebook with 90 pages of notes on Morgan, but death intervened before he could complete the project. It was instead left to his own Beaumont, Friedrich Engels, to complete the task. Engels's *Origins of the Family, Private Property, and the State*, which is subtitled *in Light of the Researches of Lewis H. Morgan*, is essentially an exegesis of *Ancient Society*. Morgan, Engels wrote, "in his own way has discovered afresh in America the materialistic conception of history discovered by Marx, . . . and in his comparison of barbarism and civilization it has led him, in the main points, to the same conclusions as Marx."[4] Chronologically, according to Morgan's system, human society has evolved through stages of savagery and barbarism, with each of those in turn divided into lower, middle, and upper "statuses" identifiable by specific attainments. The bow and arrow and pottery, for instance, demarcated the savagery-barbarism threshold, while the "Lower Status of Barbarism" ended with the domestication of animals in the eastern hemisphere and agriculture in the western hemisphere. Here, incidentally, is the precise point at which the four- and three-stage theories coalesced, as pastoralism and early agriculture were assimilated into the same "status."[5]

Although he wrote a generation after Tocqueville, Morgan's work is quite relevant to this discussion, for it quickly becomes clear to a reader of both men that they share a common structure of ideas concerning the progress of civilization. Morgan, in fact, essentially was a synthesizer of the ideas of the Scottish and French thinkers of the Enlightenment, although he contributed researches of his own. Tocqueville stands *between* the Enlightenment and Morgan, that is, between the time that a four-level theory was articulated by Smith and Millar, and the more complex three-stage classification was fixed into common parlance by Morgan.

For a long time before Tocqueville's visit, considerable attention had been paid to such stages. More than a half a century before *Ancient Society*, for example, Thomas Jefferson wrote:

Let a philosophic observer commence a journey from the savages of the Rocky Mountains, eastwardly towards our sea-coast. These he would observe in the earliest stage of association living under no law but that of nature, subsisting and covering themselves with the flesh and skins of wild beasts. He would next find those on our frontiers in the pastoral state, raising domestic animals to supply the defects of hunting. Then succeed our own semi-barbarous citizens, the pioneers of the advance of civilization, and so in his progress he would meet the gradual shades of improved state in our seaport towns. This, in fact, is equivalent to a survey, in time, of the progress of man from the infancy of creation to the present day.[6]

An even clearer example of the details of the stages is provided by the painter Thomas Cole, the leading American artist of his day, whose *The Course of Empire* series, painted during the time Tocqueville was writing *Democracy in America* (1833–36), is a vivid graphic portrayal of this process of evolution. In fact, the first three paintings of the series are visual counterparts to Morgan's categories of savagery, barbarism, and civilization, agreeing in precise detail with Morgan's later account. Cole's first painting, for example, depicted *The Savage State*. Almost as if he could have taken Morgan as his text, Cole's version of early man shows a hunter clad in skins, armed with a tell-tale bow and arrow, pursuing a deer; in the distance is a Native American–style communal teepee village. Cole's second rendering, *The Arcadian or Pastoral*, contains three essential clues to man's advanced state: agriculture, pastoralism, and stone architecture. It is an exact visual rendition of Morgan's "middle status of barbarism," which would be described with "scientific" precision more than 40 years later.

One other detail of this conception of early man required attention—the place of economic relationships in the evolution of human culture. As Arthur O. Lovejoy defined the "economic variety" of the concept of the State of Nature, it is "human society without private property, and in particular, without property in land—in other words, economic communism."[7] Tocqueville shared this particular presupposition about savages, as well: "The land is the common property of the tribe and does not exactly belong to anybody in particular," he noted (*DIA*, 323).

Morgan himself considered it "impossible to overestimate the influence of property in the civilization of mankind." Originally, he wrote, humans showed little interest in it: "The property of savages was inconsiderable. Their ideas concerning its value, its desirability and its inheritance were feeble. . . . Lands, as yet hardly a subject of property, were owned by the tribes in common."[8]

Civilization, then, could be gauged by the advancement of the idea of property. "The element of property, which has controlled society to a great extent during the comparatively short period of civilization, has given mankind despotism, imperialism, monarchy, privileged classes, and finally representative democracy." Consequently communism slowly died as civilization burgeoned, for the latter, engendered by a passion for property, intensified in its turn that very passion.

It stands to reason, then, that because human culture advances with property, civilization, the highest stage of that evolution, itself advances with the ever-ramifying complexity of property relations. Or, in the simpler words of G. T. F. Raynal, "What has assembled, clothed and civilized these peoples? Commerce."[9]

These intertwined themes of civilization and property can be followed in Tocqueville's treatment of Native Americans. The essential argument respecting the Native Americans is that they face destruction because of the calculating greed and superior firepower of the whites; but it is also that their "savage" natures make it especially difficult for them to make any viable adjustment to the whites' presence. Unacquainted with the notion of private property, they exhibit a corresponding disdain for productive labor. Ralph Lerner tersely concludes: "In the American context, this fateful disability turns out to be fatal."[10]

"When the Indians alone dwelt in the wilderness . . . their needs were few. They made their weapons themselves, the water of the rivers was their only drink, and the animals they hunted provided them with food and clothes," wrote Tocqueville of the Indian way of life (*DIA*, 321). The familiar details of this tableau alert us to the impending tragedy, for unlike Jefferson Tocqueville did not believe that neatly delineated borders separated the various degrees of human social progress. Indeed, he explicitly rejected such an image of graduated development in America in favor of a stark confrontation of the extremely advanced and the deeply retrograde.

Tocqueville described his own conclusions as having arisen out of disenchantment with the familiar Jeffersonian picture:

America, according to me, was then the only country where one could follow step by step all the transformations which social conditions have brought about for man and where it was possible to discover something like a vast chain descending ring by ring from the opulent patrician of the town right down to the savage in the wilds. It was there, in a word, that I counted on finding the history of the whole of humanity framed within a few degrees of longitude.

[But, he learned,] nothing is true in this picture. . . . The man you left behind in the streets of New York, you will find again in the midst of an almost impenetrable solitude. . . . Hence the oddest contrasts. One goes without transition from the wilds into the street of a city, from the most savage scenes to the most smiling aspects of civilization. (*J*, 355–56)

Rather than gradual transition, then, the American social landscape reveals violent contrast. Much of Tocqueville's later democratic theory would be built upon the conclusions he drew from his personal, unsettling contact with peoples who had been left behind by the trajectory of civilization's own advance from the aristocratic past to the democratic future. Such contacts made him wary, if not fearful, of the grand march of civilized life.

One other key source must be added to this catalog of influences on Tocqueville's thinking about Native Americans: his exhilarating encounter with the historical theories of the historian-statesman François Guizot, later his political adversary but nevertheless, in Alfred Cobban's estimation, "perhaps the most intelligent and high-minded minister ever to preside over the ruin of a political system."[11] From April 1829 to May 1830, Tocqueville attended Guizot's lectures at the University of Paris on the history of civilization. In August 1829, he wrote enthusiastically to Beaumont of Guizot's recently published *History of Civilization in Europe*, calling it "truly *prodigious*," and proposing that they "re-read this together this winter."[12]

Tocqueville's unmistakable sense of excitement can be felt, too, in a long letter to Charles Stoffels, one of his closest friends, in which he describes some of his ideas about civilization. One leading Tocqueville scholar, Edward T. Gargan, calls this letter "almost an explication de texte of the orientation lesson in Guizot's course of 1828," that is, the *History of Civilization in Europe*. This letter shows some doubts about civilization that predate the journey to America: "One cannot say absolutely that man becomes better in becoming civilized," he explained, "but rather that man in becoming civilized gains all at once both virtues and vices that he did not previously have."[13]

Guizot presented European history since the fall of Rome as a story of continual, if often radically uneven, progress. Naturally he had to devote a good deal of time in the early lectures to the subject of barbarism. Guizot equated barbarism with disorder; it was "the chaos of all elements, the infancy of all systems." There were in fifth-century Europe, he said, "no boundaries, no governments, no distinct people; but a general confusion of situations, principles, facts, races and languages; such was barbarous Europe." Moreover, it was a time of wandering, of semi-nomadism. "The populations were constantly being displaced, and forced one upon the other; nothing of a fixed character could be established; the wandering life recommenced on all sides."

Another aspect of the wretched state of barbarism was what would later be called *egoism*. In barbarism, liberty collapses into mere selfishness. "If men have no ideas extending beyond their own existence, if their intellectual horizon is confined to themselves, if they are abandoned to the tempest of their passions and their wills . . . no society is possible." Equally important for our purposes, then, is Guizot's explanation of the way civilization emerged out of the barbaric chaos. In the tenth century, the invasions of yet more barbarian peoples finally having ebbed, the "wandering life" ceased as well. "Populations established themselves; property became fixed; and the relations of men no longer varied from day to day, at the will of violence or chance." Guizot, in the fashion of historians of his day, entered without fear into the inner life of the people, observing that man's "ideas and sentiments, like his life, acquired fixedness."[14]

To summarize: Guizot taught that the elements of civilization were settled populations (or, in negative terms, the absence of nomadism), private property (the negation of primitive communism), and a legal system (the overcoming of anarchy); these were in turn subjectively reflected in some sort of patterned or disciplined mental life.

Before he ever departed for American shores, then, Tocqueville had certainly acquired a fairly detailed conception of the development of human culture. While in the United States, he found this heuristic structure confirmed and reinforced by his contacts with Native Americans and white settlers. The cultural advancement of a people, according to this conception, could be located on a continuum from savagery to civilization, using as evidence both artifacts and behavior. These paradigmatic assumptions were applied directly by Tocqueville when he confronted examples of socially marginal groups, particularly bondsmen, paupers, and criminals.

Tocqueville's antislavery writings reveal that he was deeply concerned, not merely with the questions of compensation to slaveholders, the transition to freedom, and the value of imports and exports of the products of slave labor, but also with the problem of ensuring the "civilizing" of colonial freedmen. This concern was in turn animated by that *mentalité*, the conceptual structure he inherited from Guizot and his century's understanding of cultural evolution, according to which slaves stood like travelers at a crossroads: they were barbarians who might either advance through the gates of civilized life or regress to a previous, savage mode of existence.[15]

Such categories, of course, were by no means always clearly delineated; they were points on a spectrum, and the transition from one stage to the next was gradual rather than sudden. Thus, the familiar phrases about former slaves "relapsing into barbarism" could plausibly be applied to areas in which plantation agriculture was most "advanced"; that is, most thoroughly commercial.[16]

And, of course, the commercial characteristic of modern civilization served as the pivotal distinction. Although the tradition was somewhat stronger in Anglo-American, than in French abolitionist thought, the notion of "the discipline of the market" was everywhere cited as a key to the advancement of blacks after emancipation. So much was riding on the proposition, including the prestige of the free-labor ideology, that when many blacks made a "retreat into self-sufficiency," rejecting "the discipline of the market," many responded by placing the blacks in a category that left them not quite human.[17]

Tocqueville did not. He saw no reason why any group of people could not reach the level of civilization. He was no racist, as his correspondence with the pioneer racist theoretician Arthur de Gobineau shows so clearly. But he was deeply Eurocentric. And the Europe of his century saw no reason to doubt its cultural superiority to technologically and socially less-developed peoples. What Tocqueville wished to do was to see to it that former slaves were forced, if need be, to advance a stage further, toward Europe—rather than backward, to the wilderness. He feared that blacks might be transformed into Indians.

Thus Tocqueville's "Report on Abolition," published just before the second volume of the Democracy, is full of concern over the civilizing process. France's intention, he wrote, must be not just liberty for colonial blacks but "civilized, industrious and peaceable societies." The blacks of the French West Indies he described as "that race oppressed and degraded by slavery which it is France's duty and honor to civilize, enlighten, and moralize, as well as enfranchise." And, perhaps most forcefully, "France labors to create civilized societies, not hordes of savages" ("Report," 115, 134, 117).

This solicitude for the civilizing process actually represented a more optimistic frame of mind than Tocqueville had manifested immediately after the journey to America. In 1833, he had expressed the fear that newly freed men and women might have to be sacrificed for the sake of their descendants. Because of the former slave's "disorderly" actions, the fact that "his passions, not progressively developed, assail him with violence"—in short, because emancipation might cause regression—

Tocqueville believed "that the transition from slavery to liberty, produces a state more fatal than favourable to the freed generation, and of which posterity alone can reap the fruits."[18] But a decade later he was sure that, given the policy of restricted landholdings, colonial blacks would not be long "in exhibiting all the tastes, and acquiring all the inclinations, of the most civilized peoples" ("Emancipation," 155).

Pauperism

A different yet closely related set of concerns is evident in Tocqueville's persistent interest in the contemporary problem of the unsettling increase in extreme poverty, a problem which, like observers of industrial development from Marx to Henry George, he linked with the increasing *aggregate* level of prosperity that accompanied the spread of market society. He was in fact among the first, and most astute, of the observers who tried to unravel the paradox of poverty and progress: "When one crosses the various countries of Europe, one is struck by a very extraordinary and apparently inexplicable sight. The countries appearing to be most impoverished are those which in reality account for the fewest indigents, and among the peoples most admired for their opulence, one part of the population is obliged to rely on the gifts of the other in order to live."[19]

So begins Tocqueville's remarkable "Memoir on Pauperism," a paper he read before the Royal Academic Society of Cherbourg early in 1835. He was at that moment in an immensely promising period of his life: not yet 30, in love with a woman of whom his family did not approve, and on the verge of a momentous trip to England, where he would be received with great deference because of the just-published *Democracy*. Yet he was, nevertheless, marked already by that seriousness of purpose and earnestness that led him to a condition of near despair about Europe's future prospects.

He had been concerned for some years about the problems of pauperism. His and Beaumont's *On the Penitentiary System in the United States* (1833) was in some respects an early foray into the problem, for pauperism and crime were closely linked issues. In *The Penitentiary System*, which contains an appendix on pauperism, the young authors had confronted the problem of the effects of the moral depravity associated with extreme want; in the "Memoir," Tocqueville attended to the causes.

On 24 March 1834, Tocqueville wrote to the English economist Nassau Senior: "I suppose that you have finished drawing up your important Report on the Poor Law. If so, I shall be much obliged if you will send me a copy through our Consul-general. The volume containing extracts from your Inquiry on the same subject has excited great interest here."[20] Senior seems to have promptly sent the promised report, and later a copy of the act itself (not passed until the following August), bearing the inscription "M. de Tocqueville from W. N. Senior."[21] Senior, a member of the great second generation of classical political economists, was the principal author of the New Poor Law, a piece of legislation he considered more significant even than the 1832 Reform Act.

The New Poor Law established a decentralized but nationally uniform system of workhouses for the indigent under the grim "Principle of Less Eligibility," according to which rigid distinctions were established between paupers and independent laborers, so as not to create incentives that might induce laborers into pauperism. Relief, therefore, was limited strictly to subsistence in a workhouse. Senior emphatically upheld the necessity of maintaining what he called "the distinction between pauperism and independence." As he wrote to an inquiring peer, "It is only by keeping these things separated, and separated by as broad and as distinct a demarkation as possible, and by making relief in all cases less agreeable than wages, that any thing deserving the name of improvement can be hoped for."[22] The poor, who did not share Senior's sanguine view of the new system, called the new workhouses "Bastilles."

Interest in English Poor Law reform was endemic among Continental liberals during the 1830s. Young Emilio Cavour, for example, composed a précis of the new legislation for the Piedmontese minister for internal affairs, and in May 1835 visited Senior at his Kensington home—only to find Tocqueville and Beaumont there already.[23] Tocqueville himself had made plans to undertake a long study of the problem in which he would propose remedies, but such plans were overtaken by other projects.

Tocqueville and Senior disagreed on several fundamental points. Cavour, who listened intently as the two older men argued the great question of wealth and poverty, recorded one of the disagreements in his diary: "An extraordinary thing was that the radical Englishman was in favour of large ownership and the legitimist [sic] Frenchman of small ownership. Mr. Senior thinks that the small proprietor has neither security nor comfort, and that it is much better for him to be in the employ of a large proprietor and have nothing to fear from bad luck or bad seasons. M. Tocqueville refuted his arguments very well both on moral and material grounds."[24]

Tocqueville perceived in England a double movement. One was a political reality, manifesting itself in a widening formal and legal equality among citizens; the other, a social phenomenon, was evident in the growing concentration of wealth. The two movements were contradictory. Some means, he told Cavour, must be sought to harmonize them. But, as Senior's views on land had demonstrated, English reformers were not of much help.

The deranged grin on the face of pauperism was one of the enduring images Tocqueville, then unknown, had taken away from his first visit to England in 1833. A London election scene—"a Saturnalia of English liberty," he termed it—left him with a sense of "disgust." Moreover, in a perceptive summary of his impressions of that visit, Tocqueville focused on the spread of pauperism as one of the most vivid. "The state of the poor is the deepest trouble of England," he wrote in his notebook. "The number of paupers is increasing here at an alarming rate." Adverting to the issue on which he would later dispute with Nassau Senior, he noted how "the number of the proletarians grows ceaselessly with the population," and attributed the increase to the concentration of wealth.[25]

During the 1835 visit, again, Tocqueville was appalled by the poverty of the world's wealthiest society. In his brilliant evocation of Manchester, he used a rhetoric of contrarieties that reveals the connection between pauperism and uncivilization. Tocqueville "tries," observes Steven Marcus, "to bring what he has seen to intelligible generality, but all he can make out are irreducible polarities."[26] In this "new Hades," Tocqueville saw, hideous paradoxes flourish. "Everything in the exterior appearance of the city attests the individual powers of man; nothing the directing power of society." "Here is the slave, there the master; there the wealth of some, here the poverty of most." And most forcefully: "Here humanity attains its most complete development and its most brutish; here civilization works its miracles, and civilized man is turned back almost into a savage."[27]

Marcus insightfully remarks of this last passage: "This is the real thing. The mind, reaching out in its perplexity, has at last discovered the means by which it can appropriate these unbearable extremities. It does so by reproducing in itself the processes that are occurring out there. . . . [T]he contradictions consist not simply in opposites but in opposites that are at the same time inseparable unifications."[28] Yet, in focusing on the structure of these sentences, Marcus ignores their manifest content. Driving this discourse of antithesis is the image of pauperism as a reversion to a previous stage of cultural development. It is important to recall that just a few months before Tocqueville entered the description of Manchester into his notebook, he had composed, in the "Memoir on Pauperism," the most sustained meditation on the subject of cultural evolution in the entire body of his work. In it, he linked pauperism to primitivism in a specific and revealing way.

As a good social scientist must do, Tocqueville opened by making explicit his theoretical assumptions. In order, he says, to explain the paradox of poverty amid progress with which the "Memoir" opens, he must "return for a moment to the source of human societies." "We see men assembling for the first time. They come out of the forest, they are still savages." The savage hordes seek only a means of ensuring life's necessities, and "if they obtain them without exertion, they consider themselves satisfied with their fate and slumber in their idle comfort" (3–4). Here we can see once more one of the essential elements of savage life, the reciprocal interaction of idleness and minimal desires. In "this first age of societies, men . . . have very few desires" (4). As he had written in the *Democracy* about the Native Americans, "their wants were few." In the "Memoir," he again drew attention to the paucity of their desires. "Lying amidst the smoke of his cabin, covered with coarse clothes . . . the Indian looks with pity on our arts, considering the refinements of our civilization as a tiresome and shameful subjugation. They envy us only our weapons," he said (4)—for, as savages, they are hunters.

With the advent of agriculture, however, humans moved to a new level of sociocultural development. "Before agriculture is known to them they live by the hunt." But with agriculture, "private property is created, and with it enters the most active element of progress." For "from the moment that men possess land, they settle" (4). Here the carefully studied lectures of Guizot, as well as the less obvious influence of the Enlightenment scheme of progress, are evident. The triad of property, progress, and settlement characterize this new level.

But these gains, while substantial, are ambiguous. "With superfluity comes the taste for pleasures. . . . The origins of almost all aristocracies should be sought in this [second] social stage." Hierarchies are created; the few begin their accumulation of power and wealth, while "the half-savage crowd" is caught "between a savage independence that they no longer desire, and a political and civil liberty that they do not yet understand" (5).

Such was the portrait Tocqueville drew of life in the savage and barbarian eras. In a passage practically out of Guizot, he then described the genesis of the Middle Ages, with its manifest inequalities, and observed: "If one looks closely at what has happened to the world since the beginning of societies, it is easy to see that equality is prevalent only at the historical poles of civilization. Savages are equal because they are equally weak and ignorant. Very civilized men can all become equal because they all have at their disposal similar means of attaining comfort and happiness" (6).

In sum, Tocqueville presented an image of cultural development as a process linked with desires and discipline. In all of history, according to his theory, personal industry is proportionate to desire. In industrial society, desires both multiply and intensify, and the definition of need changes so much that the new social order produces more paupers than older, less productive ages. Meanwhile, many men and women must labor to little avail as the new world of economic interdependence renders them increasingly vulnerable to external shocks.

Pauperism considered in the aggregate had therefore both an external and an internal manifestation. Objectively it resulted from the business cycle; subjectively, from the increase in desires. "On the one hand, among these [wealthy] nations, the most insecure class continuously grows. On the other hand, needs infinitely expand and diversify, and the chance of being exposed to some of them becomes more frequent each day" (11).

As to Tocqueville's solutions to this dilemma, it is sufficient for our purpose to note that his proposals, such as workers' savings banks, were never to be worked out, and that the major thesis of the "Memoir" is that public charity must be severely curtailed, that no French poor law be enacted establishing a right to subsistence, and that private charity would provide a bond between the recipient and the giver—or more aptly between the giving and receiving classes—that might strengthen social cohesion. Tocqueville was not the commentator to look to for paeans to state-sponsored relief.[29]

More relevant to our immediate purpose is the picture he drew of paupers as barbarians, rootless and yet not truly free. It was one that applied equally well to the former slaves in Jamaica or Barbados. The question for Tocqueville was how to bring about the integration of these people into the civilized portion of society, for their own and society's benefit.

A part of the answer, as we saw, was revealed in Tocqueville's antislavery writings, where his main concern was to ensure the freedmen's participation in the network of market relationships after emancipation.

The means he proposed to ensure this outcome was to force the former slaves, in effect, to be transformed into a proletariat, working on their former masters' estates for wages, rather than retiring from market relations and producing for their own subsistence. The solution to the danger of barbarism, then, was the labor market. Through its discipline the former slaves would be trained in the habits of freedom and wage earning, the two being facets of the same jewel.

The burgeoning industrial proletariat might be similarly disciplined if it could be shielded from the externalities of depression and unemployment, presumably by some sort of self-help operation such as savings banks.

Criminals

Closely related to paupers were criminals. Indeed, it appears that it was Tocqueville's contact in America with convicts, as much as with Native Americans and freed blacks, that first jolted him into the recognition that social problems in societies that were experiencing egalitarian leveling, a process he called *démocratie*, could be placed in the context of the great trajectory of European culture from savagery to civilization.

Tocqueville's prison investigations are often passed over as a mere "pretext" for him and Beaumont to visit America, where they could undertake their real task, the study of the customs and institutions of the American people. A letter from Tocqueville to a friend in which he says "The penitentiary system was an excuse,"[30] is generally given as the reason for this viewpoint. But the prison study, which has considerable value to this day, was of more importance than this dismissive remark indicates. Regardless of the original motives behind the research, the examination of the prison system was a fruitful one, particularly because the convicts seemed to fit the taxonomic approach so important to Tocqueville's method.

Although Beaumont wrote most of *On the Penitentiary System*, it does represent Tocqueville's views as well. Tocqueville carefully reviewed the manuscript, wrote the notes, and added several appendixes. The short "Authors' Preface" is unmistakably Tocqueville's in style and content. In it he draws the connection between crime and pauperism. In fact, if this preface did not appear between the covers of a book on prisons, one would ascribe it to a work on poverty. He regards the prison as society's attempt to deal with the results of poverty. Prisons are spoken of entirely as the terrain of the very poor. The material cause of social unrest, he says, "is the unhappy condition of the working classes who are in want of labor and bread; and whose corruption, beginning in misery, is completed in the prison."[31] *On the Penitentiary System* is thus a sort of pendant to the "Memoir on Pauperism"—the work on the effects rather than the causes of material destitution. The object of the study is to examine the possible points of contact between this American institution and French culture, so as to render the analogous French institution more efficacious.

The book has the dry tone and form of an official report. It opens with a historical chapter, followed by a balanced and informative discussion of the great contemporary debate over the merits of America's two competing systems—those of the Auburn and Philadelphia prisons. After an economic analysis of prison systems in the context of state governments' budgets, Beaumont and Tocqueville take up their main theme, the "application" of the American practice to French conditions.

The theme of the early chapters on Auburn and Philadelphia is isolation. The authors describe how, beginning in the 1780s, the Quakers, "who abhor all shedding of blood" (37), succeeded in convincing Pennsylvania to abandon flogging, branding, and executions, and gradually to substitute for these punishments confinement in absolute solitude, silence, and idleness.

This series of adjustments (for it was not a wholesale revolution) culminated in the construction of massive "penitentiaries" in the 1820s. The results were terrifying. "In order to reform [the convicts], they had been submitted to complete isolation; but this absolute solitude, if nothing interrupts it, is beyond the strength of man; it destroys the criminal without intermission and without pity; it does not reform, it kills" (41).

The response of prison reformers was to introduce the element of labor—to eliminate the idleness but retain the solitude. From this innovation the two famous "systems" diverged. In Auburn, prisoners labored communally in workshops under rules of strict silence. At night they retired to solitary cells. Philadelphia, however, clung obstinately to its system of absolute isolation. There prisoners labored in individual cells at crafts, such as cobblery, that could be performed by lone workmen.

So impartial were Beaumont and Tocqueville in their presentation of the two systems that years later Beaumont was chided in the Chamber of Deputies for not having revealed a preference. But, as he admitted later, the two did lean toward the Philadelphia system.

To their surprise, Beaumont and Tocqueville found the rules of silence remarkably well observed. In all the famous penitentiaries of America—Wethersfield, Sing-Sing, Philadelphia—they reported, "we have never been able to surprise a prisoner uttering a single word" (59). "We have often trod during night those monotonous and dumb galleries . . . we felt as if we traversed catacombs" (65).

In an eerie description of the labor at Sing-Sing, they reported utter silence as some 900 convicts broke rocks while being watched over by 30 guards. In a remark that is so characteristic of Tocqueville it must come from him, the authors noted in what the guards' control consists: "The keepers communicate freely with each other, act in concert, and have all the power of association; while the convicts separated from each other, by silence, have, in spite of their numerical force, all the weakness of isolation" (60). No wonder Roger Boesche sees the prison as "Tocqueville's model for despotism."[32]

Prisons are administered by wardens answerable to a board of supervisors or inspectors, but as in every American institution there is a higher power still: "that of public opinion" (63). Yet more than silence and isolation are wanted of prisoners; they must be productive, too. Beaumont and Tocqueville compare incentive systems in the American and European prisons, and here, too, find the American arrangements superior. A kind of task system prevails in the penitentiaries. The convict is given a required minimum output to attain, after which "he begins to work for himself" (71). In Europe, by contrast, prisoners earn a percentage from the start. This allotment, called the prisoner's pécule (savings), derives from a penal philosophy completely at odds with that of the United States, where "the principle is adopted, that the criminal owes all his labor to society" (70). Beaumont and Tocqueville present the task system as a benevolent modification of harsh but just principle, not as an incentive to greater output.

The benefits of the American system derive from that mediocrity that reigns everywhere but that sometimes produces less desirable effects. While the kind of complete moral reformation that the Quakers had hoped to induce in the convict is seldom achieved, the system is conducive to the development of good habits: "Perhaps, leaving the prison [the former convict] is not an honest man, but he has contracted honest habits" (90). In another Tocquevillian distinction, the authors note that in the American penitentiaries reformation is "accidental" (in Aristotle's sense of not being intrinsic to the system) but middling improvement is "natural" to it (89). Tocqueville would soon say the same about American democracy itself.

But the real question, of course, was the relevance of the American arrangements to French society and culture. Beaumont and Tocqueville had great respect for the system they had so carefully inspected. But they knew the obstacles to its application in France were enormous, and, in fact, nearly out of the hands of policymakers. "These difficulties are in the nature of things," they wrote, "in our customs and in our laws" (118). In particular, they believed the regimen of silence would be too much for the loquacious French to bear. "The law of silence would be infinitely more painful to Frenchmen than to Americans, whose character is taciturn and reflective," they believed (120)—or professed to. More important, they cited the high regard of Americans for religion and the rule of law as reasons for the success of the penitentiary, and pointed out that, in France, such ideas and sentiments were at a premium.

Such were the obstacles rooted in custom. But the criminal laws of France presented difficulties too. Particularly vexing was the great variety of prisons for offenders of different categories. A second point of contrast arose from the fact that American prisons derived much of their efficacy from the system of local administration, a luxury in the extremely centralized political culture of France. *On the Penitentiary System* contained a pointed contemporary political message: the grip of centralization must be loosened, so that the kind of political effervescence that they had witnessed in America could revivify French local life. Were that to happen, they wrote, "the system which we indicate would become practicable" (128). But the argument seems to lack fire. "We do not present a system. We have only started a question," they assert (130). It is not hard to discern the gradual diminishing of hope as Beaumont and Tocqueville attempt to apply what they have learned about one concrete institution in America to French conditions.

In an appendix to *On the Penitentiary System*, Tocqueville composed a sustained essay on the question of penal colonies. It addressed the issue of transporting convicts in the British manner to remote locations such as Australia or, earlier, America. Tocqueville argued against such a policy. Among the reasons was, just as in the case of freedmen, the possibility of cultural regression. In a passage reminiscent of sections of the "Report on the Abolition of Slavery," Tocqueville portrayed a savage landscape: "If the soil, on which the penal establishment is founded, presents natural resources to the isolated individual; . . . if the climate is constantly mild, wild fruits abundant, and hunting, it will be readily imagined, that a great number of criminals will profit by the half liberty left to them, to fly into the desert. . . . If the continent, where the penal colony has been planted, were peopled by semi-civilized tribes, the danger would be still

greater." Penal colonies, that is, exist in locations which induce a reversion to a hunting-gathering state. Moreover, Europeans placed among
primitive peoples "will emigrate in numbers toward the aborigines."
The criminal, although ignorant and vicious, placed by civilized policies
"on the lowest step of society, is yet first among savages." Tocqueville
characteristically included empirical evidence for such a prediction: the
mixed-race descendants of English convicts in Van Diemen's Land,
whom he portrayed as "more barbarous than the Europeans, more civilized than the savages."[33]

Thus were transported criminals, already "on the lowest step of society," that is to say, already barbaric, placed in a situation that might
encourage a backsliding toward savagery rather than advancement to
civilization. The concern is the same as that expressed for colonial slaves,
who, upon being freed, Tocqueville wrote, "may be contented with the
few transient exertions which, under a tropical sky, supply the basic
needs of man" ("Report," 117).

Unlike the freedmen and paupers, however, the convicts seem to have
no recourse to salvation through labor markets. Tocqueville and
Beaumont appear to have been every bit as stymied by the problems of
crime, punishment, and rehabilitation as our own contemporary correc-
tions experts. The attention that has been paid to the general atmosphere of optimism surrounding the great nineteenth-century penological
experiments has obscured somewhat the significance of Beaumont and
Tocqueville's own reservations about the possibilities of reintegrating
prisoners into society.

There were, then, limits to the possibilities of civilization through participation in market society. Tocqueville's power of discrimination is nowhere
more evident than in this aspect of his ambivalence about modern civilization. He had learned enough from Montesquieu to realize that civilizations
decay through their failure to renew their own vitality. When this catastro-
phe happens, he believed, modern civilization will mimic the conditions of
barbarism. The political name for this condition was despotism. Its social
name was apathy. And at the level of individual psychology, Guizot's "ideas
and sentiments," such apathy manifests itself as egoism.[34]

As Montesquieu, who along with Rousseau was the most important
political thinker in Tocqueville's intellectual formation,[35] wrote, barbarism and despotism were intimately connected. With extreme com-
pression, he expressed it thusly, in chapter 13, "The Idea of Despotism,"
in book 5 of *The Spirit of the Laws*: "When the savages of Louisiana want

fruit, they cut down the tree and gather the fruit. There you have despotic government."[36]

Roger Boesche has recently analyzed Tocqueville's fear of despotism in a way that sheds some light on the difference between paupers and prisoners. Boesche convincingly shows that the prison was in fact "Tocqueville's model for despotism."[37] He discovered in the Philadelphia prison that condition of isolation, powerlessness, and equality that would come to characterize modern despotic regimes. When Boesche's insight is seen in tandem with the cultural perspective here presented, it begins to appear probable that Tocqueville's less than optimistic attitude about convict regeneration was due to the innately regressive characteristics of the regime of prison discipline .

But in a larger sense, the isolation and equality produced by modern market societies threatened a prisonlike despotism simply by virtue their own inner tendencies. If civilization brings abundance, abundance threatens to encourage barbarism. The reason, simply put, is that the easy fulfillment of desire threatens to soften the rough edge of industry and produce lethargy. Persons may withdraw into the circle of their family and friends, leaving a vacuum in public life into which despotism may be drawn. For this danger there is but one protection—liberty: "There are many men in France who regard equality of conditions as the first of evils and political liberty as the second. When forced to submit to the former, they strive at least to escape the latter. But for my part, I maintain that there is only one effective remedy against the evils which equality may cause, and that is political liberty" (*DIA*, 513). The great tension in Tocqueville, that between democratic liberty and democratic despotism, was thus also a tension between civilization and barbarism. In the manuscript for the 1840 *Democracy*, Tocqueville posed the question directly: "I wonder if by becoming democratic [the European peoples] run the risk of falling back into a sort of barbarism."[38] If this question was less urgent for the Americans, that was because the new nation was suffused with political life on the local level and with associations for all sorts of public purposes, which kept the centrifugal forces of American life in check and the public spirit vital. For paupers, convicts and former slaves, persons with immediate contact with despotism and themselves on the cusp of barbarism, the dangers of regression were infinitely closer. For some, their own participation in market society might serve as an orientation to civilization; for others, it might be left to their children's children.

Tocqueville, as his letter to Stoffels demonstrates, knew that civilization was an ambiguous attainment. He wished to see civilization achieved by all, but only up to a point. That point was material superfluity, a point at which there were no savages, but no despotism, either.

Lynn Marshall and Seymour Drescher have written that Tocqueville "never explicitly formulated a theory of social development by stages. His interest focused on political effects and not on social causes."[39] I agree with the second sentence more than the first. Although Tocqueville's theory of development by stages was not explicit, a clear theory can, in fact, be reconstructed by examining Tocqueville's writings on outsiders and placing it in the context of the cultural theory of his day. Markets were central to his cultural theory, but he saw too that markets and the social and psychological tensions they led to could also paradoxically bring about cultural reversion.

Chapter Five

Slavery, Race, and Imperialism

Trying Not to Be Eloquent

On 14 November 1839, Tocqueville wrote to his closest English friend, John Stuart Mill:

> Today I mail you a copy of the report which I have just published, in the name of the committee appointed by the chamber, on the abolition of slavery in our colonies. You will see that, contrary to most of my colleagues, I have not tried to be *eloquent* concerning this question. I have carefully avoided irritating colonial passions, which has not prevented their newspapers from lavishing much abuse on me. But you know what colonists are; they are all alike, to whatever nation they may belong; they become raving madmen as soon as one speaks of justice to their blacks. But it is in vain; they will not succeed in making me angry, or in having me introduce violence into the discussion.[1]

Tocqueville's careful disavowal of any recourse to eloquence on the slavery question was characteristic of his approach to that issue; it was one on which he took particular pains to achieve a dispassionate tone. At the time of the letter to Mill he was in Paris, seeing the second volume of *Democracy in America* through the press. He had concluded that the Americans were in the process of developing a full-blown philosophy of self-interest. In fact, Tocqueville at that moment in 1839 could justly be called the world's leading authority on self-interest. Keenly sensitive to its demands, he knew that on the slavery issue above all others, rational persuasion based on an interest calculation was the key to constructive action. And so, although Tocqueville believed in a natural moral law and found slavery repugnant to it, he consistently avoided extended arguments based on an appeal to moral considerations, choosing instead to couch his moral views on the question chiefly in the evolving "neutral" language of political economy.

In sending a copy of his report to Mill, Tocqueville knew he could expect a degree of approval from that great economist, for the report contained a sophisticated economic analysis of slavery and an equally cogent hypothesis about the economic shape of a postemancipation society. When the report is considered alongside a series of six articles he wrote for *Le Siècle* in 1843, and his comments on slavery in the *Democracy*, a thorough economic argument regarding slavery and emancipation can be discerned.[2] By analyzing that economic argument and assessing its merits in light of the evidence, and discussing as well some nineteenth-century conceptions of civilization and cultural evolution, I hope to draw out the full meaning of Tocqueville's abolitionist ideas.

A close examination of all the relevant texts shows that the roots of much of Tocqueville's abolitionist program lie in the *Democracy*. The place to begin, then, is with the section on Native Americans at the end of the first volume of that work. This will be compared with, and seen in the larger context of, not only the segment on blacks that accompanies it, but also the works on slave emancipation that have just been mentioned and *Marie, Or Slavery in the United States* (1835), the remarkable novel by Beaumont.

Good reasons exist to include Beaumont's romantic melodrama in a consideration of Tocqueville's thought on slavery and emancipation. In the mid-1960s, in Harvard's Widener Library, Seymour Drescher discovered on the back cover of Jared Sparks's first-edition copy of Tocqueville and Beaumont's *On the Penitentiary System* (1833) an advertisement for a forthcoming joint work by the same authors on "Institutions et moeurs américains." In October 1833, Beaumont wrote to Tocqueville of "the Americans whose institutions and *moeurs* we are seeking to describe," and added, "I will not allow myself to write an idea that has not received your approval." Moreover, in his introduction to *Marie*, Beaumont referred to the novel as a study of the *moeurs* of the Americans, his companion Tocqueville having already described that nation's institutions in the *Democracy*. Tocqueville praised *Marie* lavishly in the *Democracy*. The novel, then, is much more than "the companion book to the *Démocratie*"; it is a version, more suitable in style to Beaumont's romantic temperament, of Tocqueville's own ideas of a subject to which he would have to return at a later date.[3]

In recent years, the scholarly attention devoted to Tocqueville's views on slavery has been rather modest, at least when compared to the mountainous output from other sectors of the Tocqueville industry. Most of the slavery commentary has focused on one or another of the somewhat scattered documents that comprise his full testament on the subject and tends to view the texts from a political perspective. This political analysis can be quite valuable, especially given Tocqueville's growing stature as a great political thinker of lasting importance. But such an approach tends to neglect Tocqueville's own predilection for the language of political economy when he addressed the great question of slavery and emancipation. Moreover, those writings viewed as a whole call attention to other concerns alongside the economic analysis, at least in the years just before and after Britain's final act of emancipation in 1838. These anxieties can best be condensed by the word regression: a fear that the former slaves, who were facing a momentous fork in the road of their sociocultural development, might take the wrong turn, thereby regressing to a previous stage of human development instead of advancing to the full glories of civilization—glories, it must be emphasized, that Tocqueville believed them fully capable of attaining over the course of time. As will be seen, however, after about 1840 the accumulating evidence from the British sugar colonies tended to calm those fears, and Tocqueville's analytic gaze turned more fixedly to the great question of labor itself.

Yet that uneasiness about regression occupied a fairly prominent position in Tocqueville's thinking before the results of the English experiment began to come in. Before the English data were available, he had used as his example of one possible outcome of emancipation those disquieting people with whom he had so recently come into extensive contact while in America: the Indians.

The Indians, of whom Tocqueville writes with a mixture of candor, empathy, and disgust, were to him the clearest remaining exemplifications of a "savage" way of life, in line with the three-tiered scheme of savage, barbarian, and civilized that was explained in the previous chapter. Tocqueville sketched the Native American way of life as follows: "When the Indians alone dwelt in the wilderness from which now they are driven, their needs were few. They made their weapons themselves, the water of the rivers was their only drink, and the animals they hunted provided them with food and clothes" (*DIA*, 321). Here are the elements of savagery: Native Americans were hunter-gatherers. Their way of life preceded agricultural settlement. They dressed in skins rather than "clothes," and, perhaps most telling, they were possessed of a proud independence. Barbarism, by contrast, was an intermediate stage between savagery and civilization, characterized by agriculture and settlement, but not by the restless agitation of commerce and advanced technology.

On 27 December 1831, Tocqueville had received from Sam Houston the account, alluded to in the previous chapter, explaining where the various Native American tribes belong on the scale of civilization. It fully conforms to this scheme.

When Tocqueville wrote of Indian savagery or "barbarous Africans," then, he was using terms with an explicit and commonly understood usage. When he described the Cherokees as barbaric rather than savage, it was because they were both literate and sedentary, one of the "Civilized Tribes" to be sure, but in transition thence from their savage ancestry (*DIA*, 333–35). And when in *Marie* Beaumont joined two of his chief themes—American greed and the danger of regression in the wilderness—he did so in the story of the clash between the Cherokees and the "savage" Ottawas.[4]

To understand the nature of the transformation Tocqueville believed might be wrought by slave emancipation, one must follow the tragic account of the Indians' fate given in the *Democracy*. Their history, Tocqueville recounted, took a grim and fatal turn with the advent of Europeans, who "introduced firearms, iron, and brandy among the indigenous population of North America; they taught it to substitute our cloth for the barbaric clothes which had previously satisfied Indian simplicity" (*DIA*, 321). These products (firearms, iron, and cloth) are symbolic of technological development, standing in contrast to the Native Americans' bow and arrow, stone implements, and animal skins; while the liquor replaces the natural (not cultural) sustenance, water from the brook. Thus did the Native Americans receive the gift of a multitude of new tastes—but not the knowledge of how to gratify them. Social ties among them dissolved with the pressing advance of the whites. With "famine behind them, war in front, and misery everywhere," Tocqueville believed them doomed (*DIA*, 324).

The blacks' situation presents both telling similarities and sharp contrast to that of the Native Americans—and it is precisely the condition of servitude on which the distinction turns. While the Indian occupies the "extreme edge of freedom," black slaves exist on "the ultimate limits of slavery" (*DIA*, 318). The characteristic virtues and vices of Indians derive from the fierceness of their independence and their pride. They exhibit a "childish carelessness of the morrow characteristic of savage life" (*DIA*, 326); and their febrile sense of honor causes them to retreat to the desolate forests, where they suffer great material hardship in order to escape being "servile." In his notes for the second volume of the *Democracy*, Tocqueville scratched out the term *egoism* and began to substitute *individualism* as being more suited to a description of (white) Americans' calculating self-interest.[5] Egoism he considered to be an instinctual, individualism a rational response to the environment, and thus was a way of distinguishing savages from civilized men and women. Native Americans were egoists; white Americans individualists.

But if black slaves and Indians formed opposite poles, the *free* blacks in American society "find themselves in much the same position as the natives"; indeed, they seemed destined to suffer the fate of a vanishing "tribe" (*DIA*, 350, 351). The clear trend of thought in these pages is that blacks out of slavery might be turned into Indians.

Both Tocqueville and Beaumont cited statistics to demonstrate that the mortality rate for free blacks was higher than for slaves.[6] "Many die in misery," Tocqueville observed in a passage that could be applied to either free blacks or to Indians; "the rest crowd into the towns, where they perform the roughest work, leading a precarious and wretched existence" (*DIA*, 351). Of course, the claim that the social status and material conditions of free blacks was worse than that for slaves was often put forward in the slave societies of the western hemisphere, and the relation between Europeans' ideas of Africans and of Native Americans has a long history in antislavery thought. As David Brion Davis has shown, a "double standard" that had been applied to blacks and Native Americans for two centuries showed a "tendency to dissolve" in the second half of the eighteenth century.[7] This transformation involved the assimilation of the Negro into the literary category of Noble Savage, a step made possible by virtue of his being recognized as a potential "man of feeling." It was a complex and ambivalent process undertaken by writers who themselves may not have opposed slavery.

I suggest that this turn of events in thought and feeling required a change in outlook that permitted Africans to be perceived (against all the evidence of cultural evolution as it was understood at the time) as savage rather than barbarian. In the canon of primitivism, it seems, one really did have to be a savage to be noble; there was no such person as a Noble Barbarian.

According to this version of abolitionist primitivism, what barbarized Africans was their being violently thrust into slavery; bondage served as a kind of rite de passage from savagery to civilization, a descent into hell on the way to civilized life that, in turn, required emancipation for its fulfillment. Blacks in Africa were savages in this view; in slavery, they were barbarian.

Although Tocqueville and Beaumont were born too late to embrace the tradition of the African Noble Savage, they were its beneficiaries nevertheless; for although romantic primitivism did not animate their perspective, the twin pillars of progress and civilization did. A believer in progress pays less attention to the normative and more to the descriptive elements of savagery and barbarism. Comparing the relative costs and benefits of the two earlier stages would be pointless because civilized life is immeasurably superior to either of them, and it is civilization that emancipation stands to bring about, *if* it could be done with sufficient care and reasoned planning. The stakes, then, were not simply economic or diplomatic. Only if emancipation were effected with due regard for the problems of transition could France's colonial slaves emerge into the sunlit realm of civilization; if not, the nation would have created a population of savages.

The English Example

Though in the 1839 "Report on Abolition" concerns about regression are clearly discernible, in the subsequent articles on "Emancipation" they are barely present, the ever-increasing evidence from the British colonies having shown them to be groundless: "The Negroes once free were not long in exhibiting all the tastes and acquiring all the inclinations of the most civilized peoples" ("Emancipation," 155). "The English example" could now he invoked to other purposes. "The English . . . have shown other nations what must be done," he contended, "and what must be avoided" ("Emancipation," 164, 161). The real problem by 1843 was the labor problem.

Tocqueville's starting point in the "Report on Abolition" was the experience of the British in the West Indies. There, slavery had been abolished by an act of Parliament in 1833, but the actual terms of emancipation were complex, roundabout, and, ultimately, unworkable. Parliament had legislated a six-year period of labor under their former masters for most of the former slaves. This six-year span was euphemistically termed an "apprenticeship" period because one of its objectives was to have been to introduce the blacks to freedom gradually.

But the scheme failed utterly. For one thing, as William A. Green explains, impartial almost to a fault: "a majority of the planters took an exacting, rather than a conciliatory approach to their apprentices."[8] In Britain itself, the special magistrates appointed to oversee the transition were increasingly perceived as being biased in favor of the planters. Parliament faced a snowballing opposition, particularly after two prominent abolitionists, Joseph Sturge and Thomas Harvey, published *The West Indies in 1837*, a report of their firsthand investigation that sold very briskly. In November 1837 the apprenticeship abolition movement attained an impressive degree of organization, as the Central Emancipation Committee was established at a public meeting at Exeter Hall in London. Some 30 MPs, including Daniel O'Connell, were in attendance. Hounded by abolitionist forces at home indignant at the intensification of labor and the failure of the magistrates, Parliament passed the Abolition Amendment Act in the spring of 1838, opening the door for complete emancipation. Tocqueville's "Report" was submitted only ten months after this dramatic, final deliverance.

Although the apprenticeship system as Parliament had devised it clearly had not effected a smooth transition to freedom, Tocqueville found promising elements in it. There was, especially, the idea of a fixed period of time during which those so recently in bondage could be habituated to their freedom. "It is only the experience of liberty—liberty long possessed and directed by a power at once energetic and restrained, which can prompt and form in man the opinions, virtues, and habits which suit a citizen of a free country," he believed ("Report," 102).

In fact, Tocqueville could not be firmer about this point concerning habits. "If in the course of this book," he wrote in the first volume of the *Democracy*, "I have not succeeded in making the reader feel the importance I attach to the practical experience of the Americans, to their habits, opinions, and, in a word, their mores, in maintaining their laws, I have failed in the main object of my work" (*DIA*, 308). On 13 September 1831, in Boston, the young traveler had noted in his diary the germ of another idea that takes on greater significance in the context of the writings on emancipation: "In America, free morals (*moeurs*) have molded free political institutions, in France it's for free political institutions to create the mores" (*J*, 149). "The principal object" of the *Democracy*, then, was to demonstrate the interaction of habits and free institutions; as the diary entry shows, the causes and effects of each could be hard to disentangle.

Although, as I have noted, Tocqueville used such terms as *manners*, *customs*, and *habits* almost interchangeably, these passages should serve to remind us of the importance he attached to experience and training among a free people. In Tocqueville's mind, then, the impending liberation of a quarter of a million colonial bondsmen could only be accomplished successfully by recourse to some kind of apprenticeship. But how to avoid the social and economic miscalculations that the British had made in the West Indies? This was the essential problem as he saw it, and, far from being a simple economic question, it was rather a complex moral, psychological, and social issue that, for reasons explained above, he chose to express in terms that were chiefly economic.

The Economics of Emancipation

France possessed four slave colonies, two in the Antilles (Guadeloupe and Martinique), one on the Caribbean coast of South America (Guiana), and one on the Indian Ocean east of Madagascar (Réunion, known then as Bourbon). These were sugar colonies, important sources of metropolitan revenue and, just as important, of political pressure on the July Monarchy (July 1830–February 1848). This is not to say that emancipationist forces in France were particularly radical; indeed, antislavery enjoyed the status of a sort of officially sanctioned object of social reform during Louis Philippe's reign, and abolitionist agitation came from the highest ranks of the political nation, the *pays légal*. But every move toward emancipation was subject to a dreary succession of delaying countermoves; in fact, French colonial slavery outlived the monarchy itself, dissolving in a whirlwind of unplanned political activity during the revolutionary year of 1848.[9]

Tocqueville considered slavery to be an enormous detriment to the colonies and, through them, to France herself. Its abolition would therefore benefit both the blacks and France. The planters were caught in the middle, however, incapable of accepting the actions that would advance even themselves in the long run. Unable to compete with free labor, Tocqueville thought, slavery was simply bad economics. But like many such evils, it was much easier to recognize than to eliminate.

These conclusions had emerged some years earlier from his analysis of the institution as it functioned in the United States. Although bondage cost the master very little, he had argued in the first volume of *Democracy in America*, it yielded little in return. The expenses of slavery after the initial capital investment were outlays for monitoring and maintenance, the latter including the cost of supporting the very old, the very young, the ill, and the disabled, so that the overall cost of maintenance was higher than that for any given number of productive slaves.

Free labor, in contrast, cost more, but also brought in greater profits to those who hired it. Two reasons account for this disparity: first, the free worker's higher productivity ("The free laborer . . . works faster than the slave, and the speed with which work is done is a matter of great economic importance" [*DIA*, 346]); second, the fact that he could be laid off in slack times. In short, the slaveowner dribbled out small maintenance and monitoring costs and reaped a small return, while the capitalist paid a wage greater than mere subsistence but retained much higher earnings through productivity gains and firings, so that in the end "the slave has cost more than the free man, and his labor is less productive" (*DIA*, 347). Finally, Tocqueville suggested as an additional factor in the costliness of slavery the fact that prices in the major slave entrepôt, New Orleans, were inflated by the greater profitability of sugar plantations in the surrounding region (*DIA*, 347 n. 38).

Yet, the applicability of this "free labor" analysis had its limits, for slavery did manifest some economic advantage. The products of slave labor were cultivated on large units of production that had achieved economics of scale. Tobacco could more efficiently be raised on larger units than could the cereal grains of northern agriculture; efficient cotton plantations were still larger; and (a fact of greater significance when Tocqueville turned his attention to the French colonies) sugar demanded the largest scale of all. Not surprisingly, all these commodities required southern climes (*DIA*, 352–53).

The obstacles to American abolition were both political and economic. Politically, the problem was democracy itself. Tocqueville perceived clearly that one reason the British had been able to liberate Africans in bondage was precisely because abolition had been in that instance a colonial question. In imperialist Britain, a measure of despotism made such an action possible, whereas in democratic America no real hope for freeing the slaves existed, because "it is not possible for a whole people to rise, as it were, above itself." And in the South, with its high ratio of black-to-white inhabitants, abolition was a question not of distant benevolence but of "life and death." In an observation that would later be echoed in the "Report," he remarked on the futility of even gradual emancipation in such a society because it would introduce "the principle and the idea of liberty . . . into the very core of slavery" (*DIA*, 356, 360, 354).

The economic impediment he described tersely. All the factors of production—land, labor, and capital—were monopolized by the whites: "Only descendants of Europeans own the land and are absolute masters of the whole labor force; they alone are rich, educated, and armed" (*DIA*, 355).

Such were Tocqueville's economic views on slavery in 1835. In 1839 and 1843 he returned to the subject, but on these latter occasions with different purposes. Whereas in the *Democracy* he had treated it as peripheral to his true subject, four years later his object was to persuade the

Chamber of Deputies to undertake an emancipation project. Although the economic analysis of the 1839 "Report" might plausibly be attributed to the stylistic conventions of legislative reports, the emphasis on utility is, as I have tried to show, actually quite consistent with that in the *Democracy*. In 1843 he wrote anonymously, in a newspaper of the dynastic opposition, to engender public support for emancipation. The propagandistic intent of this last series of articles partly explained the relative absence of attention to possible reservations about the liberation of the slaves, as well as the more straightforwardly political tone of the pieces. They argue for emancipation on political, even primarily nationalist, grounds, and place less stress on the economic. Nevertheless, in both these later works he became an economic forecaster, soberly trying to discern the outlines of a future without bondage.

The key postemancipation input would clearly be labor. Could the former slaves be counted upon to continue to labor in the plantation fields or would they withdraw to their small plots and produce only for their own needs? The abolitionist consensus was that they could be expected to work for wages. The reason for this belief was at bottom a simple one: they would be laboring for their own self-interest rather than for that of others. The alchemy of the market transmuted all actions into transactions. The freedmen would be no exception to this rule—for it was a rule, a law of human behavior. As Daniel O'Connell stated during the 1833 emancipation debates, "If the negro became an idler, let him share the fate of the idler—let him perish."[10] The near universality of such a belief among abolitionists is an essential starting point for understanding the emancipation debates, as well as the general abandonment of freedmen by liberal whites in the late nineteenth century.

While not so optimistic as the most sanguine of his British counterparts, Tocqueville—that most British of French abolitionists—also expected the labor supply to remain relatively inelastic. He did foresee the potential danger of a withdrawal from the labor force. The pitfall our colonies must evade, he contended persuasively, is not another Haiti but a slow degeneration: "not the violent destruction of our colonies but their gradual decay, and the ruin of their industry by the cessation, diminution, or expense of labor" ("Report," 117). Yet such a possibility did not, in 1839, appear too likely. In the British West Indies, it seemed, "the freed Negroes have nowhere manifested that predicted taste for a wandering and savage life. They have, on the contrary, appeared very attached to their original homes, and to the civilized habits they had already adopted" ("Report," 127). If a decline in labor force participation should occur, however, Tocqueville was prepared to endorse a policy of coercion. In a pivotal section of the "Report," he spoke bluntly. "If it be thought necessary to colonial production, and to the continuation of the white race in the Antilles, that the services of the enfranchised Negro be permanently available for hire by the great proprietors, it is evident that we should not allow him a plot where he can easily live by laboring only for himself" ("Report," 129). But an important point to note about this sentence is that it is written in the subjunctive: *If* the blacks withhold the labor so crucial to France's colonial position, then alternatives to such labor should be prohibited.

This passage also points to the significance of the second factor of production, land, and to its inextricable connection with labor. Tocqueville foresaw that the former slaves could become small proprietors and still labor for wages. In other words, land availability by itself need not hinder output. Indeed, the image of such small proprietors producing for the market was reminiscent of France ("Report," 129). Still, it was potentially dangerous because sugar is the crop most in need of economies of scale. Small peasants on the French model could not replicate the plantation-factories of Antigua, Barbados, or Jamaica.

Tocqueville saw that the land-labor ratio would be crucial to labor force participation, and that it would therefore be the key to wages. Because it was anticipated that former slaves would become wage earners, what sort of wage could they expect to receive? Or, to put it another way, what would emancipation cost the planters, and how would the flow of those expenditures change over time? Tocqueville expected a temporary disequilibrium, as wages would rise above the subsistence the slaves received at the time; but this surge in wages would be followed by productivity gains that would cover those higher wage levels.

It was this disequilibrium period that justified Tocqueville's recommendation that the planters be compensated—not the notion of replacing the slaves as property. Even a decade later, when he sat on the commission to determine the slaveowners' compensation, he was instrumental in having the commission stick to this distinction. Thus it was the loss of labor, not of capital, for which the planters were being indemnified: "From the outset your Commission rejected the idea of assimilating slave property to other kinds of property protected by law. They do not admit that restoring liberty to a Negro is parallel to the State's seizing property for the public good. Man has never had the right of possessing man, and the possession itself has always been and still is unlawful" ("Report," 111).

This finely drawn, but erroneous, distinction reveals Tocqueville momentarily dropping his pose of dispassionate calculation and exposing his moral sensibilities. Slaves being a form of human capital-in-labor, it makes little difference whether their owners are compensated for the loss of their capital or of their labor. Providing the planter with the purchasing power to pay the former slaves wages over a designated period of time is analytically the same as purchasing them as capital goods.[11]

Thus the moral case for compensation. The specifically economic argument was that planters required help if former slaves' wages *"exceed* the sum for which their cooperation could be compelled during slavery" ("Report," 112; emphasis added). That sum, it will be recalled from the discussion of slavery in the *Democracy*, Tocqueville had computed as the cost of maintenance (including that of the unproductive) plus monitoring. In theory, a worker in a competitive wage system receives the value of his marginal product, and it is precisely the difference between that value and the cost of monitoring and maintenance that represents the slaveowner's exploitation of his bondsmen. But if, after slavery, wages do measure up to the value of the marginal product, and at the same time do not exceed the former monitoring-maintenance costs (as Tocqueville thought they should not), the unproductive clearly will have disappeared from the equation. To put it another way, it ought to be expected that the workers' aggregate wages would be sufficient to maintain the aggregate black population—the children and the elderly, the ill and the disabled, as well as the workers themselves—at a subsistence level. This, in short, is what Tocqueville expected to happen in the middle term. In the long run, he thought, productivity gains would increase prosperity for both Europeans and Africans.

But as noted above, the short run presented difficulties, and time was needed before productivity reached equilibrium with wages. While the economic system experienced the turbulence of the search for equilibrium—that is, while wages exceeded productivity—planters should receive enough to make up the difference.

As important as his predictions about wages, then, was his expectation that output would increase over time, cultivation being "more productive . . . with the labor of enfranchised Negroes, than with that of slaves. . . . We may then conclude that the revolution effected in our islands will be as prosperous for the planters as for the Negroes; and that when it is finished it will cost the proprietor less to work his fields with a small number of laborers, paid according to their work, than it presently costs him, obliged as he is to purchase and to support a host of slaves on an annual basis of whom a large portion are always unproductive" ("Report," 113).

The failure of the British emancipation plans to provide for such political and economic changes as Tocqueville wished for, as well as the urgency of the task of training freed men and women for liberty, led him to advocate what at first seems a radical alternative to the British apprenticeship. He proposed a form of state socialism, the complete severance of the link between slave and master, and the interposition of the state between the two. "The bond which now exists between them should be entirely destroyed. The State should become the sole guardian of the enfranchised population" ("Report," 132). For this plan he put forward both an economic and a political reason: the state was to act as the protector of the former slaves, paying them their wages while withholding a portion as an indemnity for the planters. In this manner, the newly liberated blacks would be forced to look to the state for succor and, in the process, be trained in the proper habits of civilization and liberty. This regimen would involve the government's "founding an empire over the minds and habits" of the blacks, and avoiding the British error of failing "to instill competitiveness among them" ("Report," 131).

But the assumption that emancipated slaves would stay on the plantations and continue to work for wages was a central miscalculation of abolitionists in all the Atlantic world. Planters had always claimed to know otherwise, and they proved, in time, to have been the superior economic forecasters. For the supply of labor turned out to be very elastic indeed, as former slave women and children left the fields, and men, women, and children showed a marked preference for economic self-sufficiency over production for market. Planters, then, had to face the reality of what economists call the "backward-bending supply curve" of labor—as freed men and women sought to enjoy the gains of freedom rather than maximize money income. The economic result was a drastic decline of sugar output wherever sufficient land existed to provide the former slaves with an alternative to plantation labor. The struggle over control of land and labor is tersely summarized by Herbert S. Klein: The ex-slaves "would work on the old plantations for their ex-masters only if they could not get access to their own lands or if they could find no alternative employment, urban or otherwise. If given no opportunities or land, they still refused to return to the old plantation working conditions. They demanded immediate withdrawal of their wives and daughters from field labor, an end to gang-labor arrangements, payment in money wages for all labor, and access to usufruct land for their own cultivations."[12]

Tocqueville's errors, although a matter of degree, were nonetheless serious. They may be said to typify the classic shortcoming of economic prognosticators before and since, inaccuracy in forecasting elasticities. By 1843, then, the emerging picture of emancipation in the British West Indies was distressing to many abolitionists. The evidence showed that the labor force had abandoned the planters. "Every ounce of British cupidity and activity" was being stretched to obtain workers. Meanwhile, wages, the very badge of freedom, had risen faster than the price of sugar, as the former slaves exhibited a tenacious reluctance to become a rural proletariat. Restricting land availability was now seen as imperative. The policy Tocqueville had only conditionally proposed in 1839—"if it be thought necessary to production that the Negro's services be permanently available for hire . . . [then] we should not allow him a plot [of land]"—became the centerpiece of his Le Siècle series. In these articles, the subjunctive mood was abandoned in favor of the indicative: "A temporary prohibition on landholding will apparently not only be the most effective of any of the possible exceptional measures, but actually the least oppressive as well" ("Emancipation," 142, 156, 166).

Thus would the modern-day Hercules unbend the backward curve of the recalcitrant supply of labor. The training for freedom for the liberated slaves paradoxically entailed a limitation of freedom.

Seymour Drescher has observed that Tocqueville's desire, like that of other abolitionists, was to "have artificially proletarianized and Europeanized" colonial blacks. For, in Thomas C. Holt's cogent words, "The problem was not merely to make ex-slaves work, but to make them into a working class."[13] Consideration of this fact leads us to a brief examination of the third factor of production, capital. Tocqueville made two arguments about this factor. First, determining who owned what in the colonies was impossible because the lands were hopelessly encumbered with mortgages. Tocqueville wanted to see a general "compulsory expropriation" by the government to "bring the true proprietors to light" ("Emancipation," 168). Second, insecurity about the future of slavery had inhibited the planters from making improvements. "The uncertainty of their approaching destiny weighs heavily upon the colonies; it contracts their intelligence and abates their courage" ("Report," 104; see also "Emancipation," 141). (Although Tocqueville professed to eschew eloquence, he could not always abandon to the demands of a dry objectivity his genius for the vital phrase.)

He expected, however, that abolition would remove the uncertainty, causing planters to add to their fixed capital. As a consequence, the infusions of both free labor with its greater productivity, and capital improvements, would result in higher output. The outlook, then, with luck, with prosperity and stability as a context for emancipation, and with the aid of a stringent tariff, was for civilized advancement in the colonies ("Report," 114; "Emancipation," 168).

The abolition of slavery was, therefore, both moral and economic in scope; inevitable yet hazardous in execution. The first of two prominent links between the economic and the moral was the land-labor ratio. It will be recalled that the availability of land was recognized as a vital factor in the ex-slaves' potential productivity. Planters had no question about the connection. "Emancipation," writes the historian James L. Roark, "confronted planters with a problem their deepest convictions told them was impossible to resolve—the management of staple-producing plantations employing free black labor."[14] But why was this their conviction? Partly because planters knew full well the intensity of the labor that they were able to obtain by organizing labor in gangs; but also because of the disquieting similarity of the slave societies to savage landscapes. This was particularly the case in the West Indies, where "planters would continually ask, what disciplinary force would keep the Negro at work in a tropical climate where food could easily be grown or even picked from trees?"[15] A frank expression of this uncertainty appears in a memorandum prepared by an official in the British Colonial Office, Henry Taylor, in 1833. If the slaves after emancipation need work only two days on their provision grounds in order to subsist, he asked, "what, except compulsion, will make them work six?" He articulated the fear of regression—that former slaves may fall "into a barbarous indolence" and live as hunter-gatherers, "like beasts in the woods."[16] The theme occurs prominently in Tocqueville's "Report" as well: "We must anticipate that they . . . may be contented with the few transient exertions which, under a tropical sky, supply the basic needs of man." Yet "France labors to create civilized societies, not hordes of savages" ("Report," 117)—that is, quite literally, of hunter-gatherers clad in skins.

The second major connection between economics and morality can be seen in Tocqueville's discussion of honor and the related notion of the dignity of labor. Like other economists, Tocqueville argued that slavery confers dishonor on all labor. "All travelers in slave societies," he modestly observed in his "Report," "have perceived that the idea of labor is inseparably connected with the idea of servitude. Labor is not only

avoided as a painful effort, but shunned as a dishonor" ("Report," 107).
He himself had expressed this perception in his well-known description
of the journey down the Ohio, with a slave state to his left and a free one
to the right. Sounding like Samuel Clemens on the Mississippi north of
Cairo, he wrote:

> The traveler who lets the current carry him down the Ohio till it
> joins the Mississippi sails, so to say, between freedom and slavery; and he
> has only to glance around him to see instantly which is best for mankind.
> On the left bank of the river the population is sparse; from time to
> time one sees a troop of slaves loitering through half-deserted fields; the
> primeval forest is constantly reappearing; one might say that society had
> gone to sleep; it is nature that seems active and alive, whereas man is idle.
> But on the right bank a confused hum proclaims from afar that
> men are busily at work; fine crops cover the fields . . . man appears rich
> and contented; he works. . . .
> On the left bank of the Ohio work is connected with the idea of
> slavery, but on the right with well-being and progress; on the one side it
> is degrading, but on the other honorable. (*DIA*, 345–46)

The central point of this contrast is that honor is rendered to labor as
such in free society. That was why Tocqueville insisted that making not
only economic but also moral preparations for emancipation was necessary. Slaves had no reason to suppose that labor conferred honor and dignity, or that freedom, civilization, and labor were inextricable. Were they
not to receive such guidance, such training for liberty, emancipation
must fail. Thus, even a sort of Rousseauian coercion was justifiable. The
state should, he argued, "first *show* him and then, if necessary, *pressure*
him into the arduous and manly habits of liberty"; but later in the
"Report" he has the state "*impose* those conditions which it may judge
indispensable, and *compel* their submission" ("Report," 117, 133; emphasis added).
Tocqueville's arguments about slavery certainly do tend to demonstrate a notion of freedom that seems limited by our advanced lights.
There is therefore some irony in fact that they are rooted, like so much
else in his life, in that seminal journey to the laboratory of equality, the
United States. Yet they exhibit that intellectual honesty, openness to the
evidence, and penchant for gradual modification so characteristic of all
his work as a social scientist.
But, of course he was much more than a social scientist; he was a
moralist as well. And nowhere are his moral preoccupations clearer, and

the results more ambivalent, than in his attempts to grapple with imperialism.

Tocqueville in Canada and Algeria: Dilemmas of Scientific Racism

That race, as such, has no concrete existence, is a fact central to our contemporary moral consciousness. Racial awareness arose in its modern, virulent form in the nineteenth century with the rise of positivism and scientism and their demand to accept as real only that which could be measured. With the action of this demand came, in one of the many ironic reversals of nineteenth-century thought, an equal and opposite reaction. That reaction was the process we call *reification*: the attempt to treat as measurable—and therefore physically real—the manifold phantasms and projections of human culture. If the nineteenth century was, as Robert Nisbet truly says, an age rich in reifications, that was because it was also the age of science.[17]

Preeminent among these ersatz reified "things" was the one we call *race*. From the viewpoint of the life sciences, this concept is a pseudoscientific counterfeit. Its bogus nature has been well-summarized by Stephen Jay Gould, who writes: "People are so similar genetically [that] previous claims for a direct biological mapping of human affairs have recorded cultural prejudice and not nature. . . . The classical arguments of biological determinism fail because the features they invoke to make distinctions among groups are the products of cultural evolution."[18] There is, then, no such "thing" as race. From the viewpoint of the life sciences, it is as unreal and ghostly as a deluded person's hallucination.

Yet many things of this kind do exist, although they might lack measurable attributes; they just exist in a different sort of way. They can be facts of a different order of reality. For example, they can be what Emile Durkheim termed *social facts*. Durkheim defined them as "ways of acting, thinking and feeling, external to the individual and endowed with a power of coercion by reason of which they control him."[19] Race is perhaps the preeminent social fact of the last century and a half, not only in the West, but in the world. It has served to deprive whole nations of their understanding of the fundamental unity of the human race.

If the foregoing remarks seem commonplace, that is in part because we know the utter scientific groundlessness of categories of racial hierarchy. It is, in one very limited sense—a purely intellectual sense—easy for us to be against racism, because we know it lacks a scientific basis.

But what if we lived in a world in which the scientific status of racial theories were an accepted field of inquiry, or, at the least, the object of serious scientific controversy? What would ground our moral stand against racism if the scientific jury on the inequality of races were still out? Tocqueville presents us with a case study of one man's response to precisely that situation. In this section, I examine Tocqueville's reaction to the inception of the modern, "scientific" kind of racism. By doing so, I can also suggest a solution to a problem in Tocqueville scholarship that stems from any consideration of his writings on imperialism and the Algerian conquest.

Tocqueville was a voyager. From his adolescence onward, his life was punctuated by decisive journeys. At 20, as we have seen, he traveled with his brother to Sicily, and his diary and notes on that excursion reveal themes that would stay with him forever: the durability of national character, the evolution of culture, the role of religion in society. When he embarked for the United States, he was but 25 years old; *Democracy in America*'s first volume was published before his thirtieth birthday. Between the publication of the first and second volumes of the *Democracy*, he visited England, a land to which he would return on two other occasions.

Of particular importance in the development of his thought, as well as of his political career, were his excursion, during the American visit, from Detroit to Quebec via Sault Ste. Marie and Niagara Falls, and a hazardous journey ten years later to Algeria. The records of these expeditions reveal Tocqueville's unusually deductive mind attempting to establish premises about the possible links among race, national character, civilization, and liberty. The principles once discovered were starkly exposed toward the end of his life in the remarkable epistolary dialogue he conducted with Count Arthur de Gobineau, the first major exponent of a scientific racism.

The first of these two journeys, the Canadian one, helped Tocqueville formulate a thesis about the enduring nature of national character. Having wandered through the wilderness as far as Saginaw, Tocqueville and Beaumont were about to turn south, when they were presented with a chance to take a steamer from Detroit to Buffalo and thence to Montreal. They seized the opportunity for a visit to those northern parts with their French population. Since the 1790s, Canada had been divided into Upper and Lower provinces, with the French population concentrated in Lower Canada, and particularly in Montreal and Quebec.

Canada was a revelation to Tocqueville, for there he found, as if preserved in amber, the "Old France" of Louis XIV. After several months
among the people he always called "the Anglo-Americans," Tocqueville
could not conceal an almost boyish delight in the people he found in
Canada. "I tell you that you can't dispute them their origin. They are as
French as you and I," he wrote a friend. "They even resemble us more
closely than the Americans of the United States resemble the English. I
can't express to you what pleasure we felt on finding ourselves in the
midst of this population. We felt as if we were home. . . . Old France is
in Canada; the new is with us."[20] In his notebook he jotted: "Canada is
beyond comparison . . . that [part of America] which bears the greatest
analogy to Europe and, especially, to France." Between Montreal and
Quebec, he noted, "the villages we saw in the surroundings are extraor-
dinarily like our beautiful villages. Only French is spoken there. The
population seems happy and well-off. The race is notably more beautiful
than in the United States." And some days later, still astonished, "*All in
all*, this people is prodigiously like the French people. Or rather, these
still are the French people, trait for trait" (*J*, 187, 197–98).

What Tocqueville found was a Weberian "ideal type" of the French
people, absolutely pristine and unblemished in their new surroundings.
It secured in his mind the notion of the sheer perdurability of national
character.

In fact, however, the two inquirers had been prepared to reach precisely those conclusions by their experiences just before the Canadian
venture, during their perilous wilderness trek to the mosquito-infested
Michigan timberland. These events have been preserved in Tocqueville's
marvelous "A Fortnight in the Wilds."

At Saginaw a few weeks earlier, Tocqueville and Beaumont had happened upon a microscopic cultural crossroads, an entrepôt of American,
French, and Indian ways of life consisting of but 30 people. To their surprise, they found that the three groups shared absolutely nothing in common. "Chance, interest or desire had brought together these thirty people
in this narrow space. There was no other common link between them,
and they were profoundly different. One found French Canadians there,
some Americans, some Indians, and some half-castes," he recounted, and
then in his customary fashion drew a general conclusion: "Some philosophers have believed that human nature, everywhere the same, only varies
according to the institutions and laws of different societies. This is one of
the opinions to which the history of the world seems to give the lie on
every page. In history all nations, like individuals, show their own pecu-

liar physiognomy. Their characteristic traits reproduce themselves through all the transformations that they undergo. . . . Something inflexible shows through in spite of all man's adaptability" (*J*, 392).

The seeds of Tocqueville's Canadian observations, then, had been sown earlier at that forlorn Saginaw outpost. They bore fruit a few months later. In January 1832, his diaries record some thoughts that to François Furet constitute the thesis of "a national character exterior or preexistant [*sic*] to the social circumstance," a character with "an ethnic and virtually presocial foundation."[21] In that diary entry, Tocqueville composed the *bon mot* that was later to appear in the *Democracy*, that the American is the Englishman left to his own devices (*J*, 179). Anglo-Americans, it would thus seem, are to the English as the French-Canadians are to the French. And, just as the Canadians personify the "Old France" that existed prior to the upheavals of 1789, so also do the Americans exhibit the true—that is, the primitive, presocial—English character.

Such a conclusion might seem at first to be a variant of race thinking. But it would be dangerously ahistorical for us to rush to such a verdict. In 1832 terms such as *nation, tribe*, and *race* were in almost interchangeable use. Both the *Oxford English Dictionary* and its French counterpart, the *Dictionaire alphabétique et analogique*, record the usage of the word *race* as originally meaning descendants from a common ancestor, then tribe or nation, and only fairly recently formal biological groupings within the human species. Such formal systems of racial hierarchy had yet to be devised in 1832. Moreover, Tocqueville continually reiterated his abhorrence of deterministic theories of whatever sort.

It was not race, but cultural evolution, that was decisive. And decisive to cultural evolution, in turn, was the exercise of a people's liberty. Sometimes, Tocqueville thought, great nations even had to employ their liberty in the cause of destroying the freedom of others. Such was his unshakable judgment regarding Algeria. As Michael Hereth has shown, Tocqueville's convictions concerning the Algerian question did undergo a transformation from 1837 to 1847.[22] But he never wavered on the question of France's need for an Algerian conquest. Indeed, he considered it France's most important goal. Why? Because of what I consider the deepest dread in Tocqueville's mind: that of a political lethargy or enervation of spirit, an absence of passion without which a people will sink into a barbarous torpor.

As it happens, there was a widely held stereotype for such enervation—one, moreover, that linked fatalistic attitudes with a specific non-

European group. That was the image of the Muslim. It is instructive to contrast the present-day Western stereotype of the violent, fanatical disciple of Allah determined to remake the world to its nineteenth-century counterpart. Among Europeans 150 years ago, Islam was thought to induce in its adherents a complete surrender of the will that was reflected in an utterly fatalistic bearing toward life. Actually, this popular image of the Muslim persisted as late as World War II. According to Bruno Bettelheim's firsthand account, inmates at Dachau referred to those among themselves who had given up hope, and who consequently would die very soon, as *Musselmänner* (Muslims), "because of what was erroneously viewed as a fatalistic surrender to the environment, as Mohammedans are supposed to blandly accept their fate."[23]

Tocqueville was perhaps more vulnerable to the power of such an image than any of his contemporaries. The bland acceptance of fate held for him a fascination born of horror. His entire paradigm of despotism in *Democracy in America* was based on it. It explains as much as any single factor the difference in the two volumes of that work, published five years apart, in 1835 and 1840, for during those years, as Tocqueville read the situation, the French had turned toward a social and political apathy: there were none of those associations, no new political parties, none of that continual agitation so characteristic of the American society and polity that he hoped to see emerge in France.[24]

So when Tocqueville, by then a deputy for Valognes and a recognized authority in the Chamber on colonial questions, visited Algeria in 1841, he was aghast not at the depredations of the unmanageable French forces, but rather at the seeming decadence of the Arab and Kabyle tribes. Two years later he wrote to Gobineau, "I often studied the Koran when concerned with the Moslem populations of Algiers and the Orient. I must say that I emerged convinced that there are in the entire world few religions with such morbid consequences as that of Mohammed. To me it is the primary cause of the now visible decadence of the Islamic world. . . . I still regard it as decadent compared to antique paganism."[25]

"Let us not, in the middle of the nineteenth century, repeat the history of the conquest of America," Tocqueville beseeched the Chamber of Deputies in his 1841 "Report on the Algerian Question."[26] But his later actions and writing disclose a willingness to employ any means the Army thought necessary to complete the conquest, including the infamous *razzia*, an instrument of terror inflicted on native villages that proved a worthy forebear of such twentieth-century descendants as the "strategic" bombing of civilian targets in World War II. Indeed one is forced to agree with Melvin Richter's conclusion that Tocqueville's dramatic warning lacks sincerity.[27] As Michael Hereth has well said, "any admirer of Tocqueville is baffled" by the Algerian writings.[28] They seem in fact to be negations of the ideas of ordered liberty that characterized the *Democracy*, the second volume of which was published just one year before the Algerian report.

"Tocqueville," Hereth writes, "never applied his knowledge of the evil consequences of foreign rule to Algeria" because he saw it as an entirely French affair.[29] But I believe there is another reason, linked to the fear of social and political paralysis: the fatalistic Algerians presented a danger of contamination to the already lethargic French polity.

In 1837, Tocqueville, in his earliest writings on the question, had advocated racial intermarriage as a means to the ultimate goal of "a mixed-race society, which would erect a great monument to the glory of our fatherland on the coast of Africa"[30]—clear evidence of the absence of racism in his thinking. But by 1841, he considers conquest the only practical goal of French policy. Race-mixing with members of an inferior, because fatalistic, civilization would only spell disaster to a France that was even then devoid of political passions and sinking into the mire of despotism.

That despotism arrived sooner than nearly anyone except Tocqueville had predicted. With the destruction of the 1848 constitution and the establishment of the pompous dictatorship of Napoleon III, Tocqueville was yet again proved right. Before the coup, however, Tocqueville served a brief five months as France's foreign minister. During this time, his secretary was an ambitious and somewhat fawning young aristocrat, Arthur de Gobineau, whom he had met some six years earlier, probably through the intercession of some of his royalist friends. Gobineau and Tocqueville's correspondence comprises a remarkable "dialog between archetypes"[31] in which the believer in liberalism, democratic order, and stitutionalism confronts the materialist, determinist, in short "scien-
," proponent of racism. Curiously, however, the eloquent arguments of Tocqueville in this great correspondence are almost wholly at odds with his prescriptions for the inhabitants of Algeria.

Gobineau's scientific pretentions are everywhere evident. In 1856, after years of epistolary wrangling over the matter, an exasperated Gobineau wrote: "What disturbs me is that you, monsieur, who do like me, maintain a reserve about the very morality of my concepts. What can I say to you? If truth and morality are not connected, I shall be the first to agree that my book is devoid of the latter, but then it is also

devoid of anti-morality, as are geology, medicine, archaeology. My book
is research, exposition, presentation of facts. These facts exist or they
don't. There is nothing else to say" (286).

Tocqueville's bitter antagonism toward Gobineau's theories had moral
and religious roots. Nothing could make him budge from the truth, what
must be called in context the revealed truth of the oneness of the human
race, regardless of the putatively scientific claims of Gobineau. He
assailed Gobineau's logic as well, nowhere more cogently than in a magnificent letter of 17 November 1853. Your doctrines, he wrote, "would
lead [your readers] straight from races to individuals and from social
capacities to all sorts of potentialities." Their consequence is "a vast limitation, if not a complete abolition, of human liberty." In a sentence, he
shattered the pretentions to scientific method: "No one will be able to
prove it since to do so one would need to know not only the past but also
the future. I am sure," he continued, "that Julius Caesar, if he had had the
time, would have readily done a book to prove that the savages he had
encountered on the island of Great Britain were not at all of the same
human race as the Romans and that, whereas the latter were destined by
nature to dominate the world, the former were destined to vegetate in a
corner (227–28). Thus did Tocqueville reiterate the conception he had
formed a quarter of a century earlier, in a youthful essay on English history: "After all rational equality is the only state natural to man."[32]

Most of all, however, Tocqueville based his opposition to Gobineau's
racism on the grounds that it was fatalistic. "It promotes the spiritual
lassitude of your already weakening contemporaries," he contended
(232). It is "like opium given to a patient whose blood has already weakened" (270). For "Our [French] temper . . . is now going through a
transformation which is manifest in lassitude, in disenchantment, in a
dislike of ideas, in a love of statistics. . . . How can you expect a book like
yours . . . to disturb the deep, lethargic sonmolence which is now weigh-
ing down the French spirit?" (292–93).

Tocqueville, therefore, rejected the first signs of scientific racism for
some of the same reasons he supported the violent, racist domination of
the Arab and Kabyle tribes of North Africa: a liberty that was contingent upon a kind of political ebullience could countenance neither a theory nor a people whose inclination was toward quietude.

Chapter Six
Revolutions, Past and Future

In the last years of Tocqueville's life, France was ruled by a despot, Louis Napoleon Bonaparte, known as Napoleon III, who was the nephew of the greater tyrant whose name he shared and whom Victor Hugo famously branded "Napoléon le petit." Napoleon III seized power in a coup d'état in December 1851, thereby abruptly terminating the short-lived Second Republic that had been born amid the turbulence of the Revolution of February 1848. Tocqueville contemplated this calamity with that mixture of passion and detachment that imparts such an eloquent tension to the best of his works. Once again he was forced to ponder modern man's abandonment of liberty—always, as Alan Kahan notes, a more salient theme in his work than its acquisition.[1]

Both processes—the forsaking of freedom and Tocqueville's meditation on it—began with the Revolution of 1848. About a year after the overthrow of the monarchy, Tocqueville accepted the post of minister of foreign affairs in the second ministry of Odilon Barrot (1791–1873). The ministry was a brief one, lasting just five months. It fell on 31 October 1849. The following summer, at his estate in Normandy, Tocqueville began writing his great memoir, the *Souvenirs* (Recollections) of the revolution and of his subsequent duties as foreign minister. These recollections, in turn, would lead him to take up once again a project he had begun in 1836 and then abandoned: a history of the French Revolution itself.

The story of Tocqueville's works on the French Revolution is complicated both by Tocqueville's own alternative commitments and by the vicissitudes of publication and translation. In 1836, between volumes 1 and 2 of *Democracy in America*, Tocqueville had contributed to John Stuart Mill's new quarterly, the *London and Westminster Review*, an essay called "The Social and Political Condition of France before and after 1789."[2] Mill translated it himself. That text would appear with little change in *The Old Regime and the French Revolution* 20 years later. In 1850, Tocqueville began the *Recollections*. It was his way of coming to terms with the seeming betrayal of the emancipatory promise of the revolution—and not only the Revolution of 1848, but that of 1789, for "there is only one [revolution]," he wrote, "which still goes on and is not yet near its end."³ Sickly and idle, yet restless and ambitious, Tocqueville after completing the *Recollections* cast about for a way to add to his reputation—for, as he wrote to Beaumont, "I tremble in advance when I think how very necessary success is for me."⁴

Yet it was not mere ambition that led him to choose the Revolution of 1789 as his subject. The thinking process stimulated by his composition of the *Recollections* also influenced him to seek the roots of the French loss of freedom in the tumultuous events of 60 years before. Moreover, as is plain to any reader of *Democracy in America*, the problem of revolution was a perennial one for Tocqueville. There is this important difference between the two books, however: whereas in the *Democracy* revolution is used chiefly to classify democratic regimes by their origins, in later years Tocqueville turned to it as a subject in its own right. This was a shift in his work that issued, François Furet notes, "not from a love of the past but from his sensitivity to the present."⁵

Once begun, the project expanded. Tocqueville published *The Old Regime and the French Revolution* in 1856, with an awkward awareness of the fact that in the book he had actually said almost nothing about the French Revolution itself. In his "Foreword" he wrote, "This book, in my opinion, calls for a sequel and I propose, if my health permits and I have the leisure, to follow it up with another."⁶ The various hesitations in this sentence ("in my opinion," "if I have [time]," "if . . . health permits") hint at the ultimate fate of that incomplete later study. In the remaining two and a half years of his life, Tocqueville made many notes and wrote drafts of several chapters, but the projected second volume was never published.

The Old Regime is available in English in a translation by Stuart Gilbert that leaves much to be desired. Gilbert, a noted literary figure in his own right, is perhaps best known as a close friend of James Joyce. Gilbert translated *Ulysses* into French and wrote *James Joyce's Ulysses*, an indispensable companion to that incomparable novel. His translation of *The Old Regime* is brisk, spirited, and frequently inaccurate. With regard to painstaking attention to details, Gilbert, it seems, was more adept at translating in the other direction.

The notes and drafts for Tocqueville's projected second volume were edited by André Jardin and published in 1953 as volume 2, part 2, of Tocqueville's complete works. From this raw material, John Lukacs tried to weave a connected narrative in his 1959 Anchor Books edition, *"The European Revolution" and Correspondence with Gobineau*. It is a readable trans-

lation that provides a lucid indication of where Tocqueville was going in
the second volume. But it was not until 1987 that R. R. Palmer, the distinguished Princeton historian of the French Revolution, furnished a
translation of Jardin's 1953 volume, with all the variants, marginal notes,
sketches, and so forth.[7] It gives the English reader not only the Jardin
text, but also insightful notes and an excellent introduction. Currently,
Alan Kahan is preparing a comprehensive translation of all the relevant
writings—both *The Old Regime* and the drafts for the following volume.
Soon the works on the French Revolution should be as easily available to
English readers as *Democracy in America* has been since 1945.

Tocqueville succinctly presents his thesis on the French Revolution at
the outset of *The Old Regime*: "The French in 1789," he writes in the
"Foreword," "spared no pains in their endeavor to obliterate their former
selves." But "they were far less successful in this curious attempt than is
generally supposed. . . . Though they had no inkling of this, they took
over from the old régime not only most of its customs, conventions, and
modes of thought, but even those very ideas which prompted our revolutionaries to destroy it; . . . in fact, though nothing was further from
their intentions, they used the debris of the old order for building up the
new" (vii). For all its violence and agitation, then, the Revolution was
less the overturning than the fulfillment of the Old Regime.

Tocqueville's research revealed that nineteenth-century administrative
practices widely believed to have originated with the Revolution and
Napoleon had actually resulted from a long-term trend toward centralized administration instituted by the monarchy. In the mid-eighteenth
century, Tocqueville found, "the government of France was already highly centralized and all powerful; indeed, the range of its activities was
prodigious. . . . Its influence made itself felt at every turn, not only in the
management of public affairs but also in the private lives of citizens and
families" (ix).

But this "Foreword," like the "Author's Introduction" to *Democracy in
America*, contains a credo as well as a thesis. Only freedom, Tocqueville
warns again, can protect a people whose aristocracy has been destroyed.
The greatest ally of despotism is self-interested cupidity. Because aristocratic states, for all their vices, served to nurture "ties of family, of caste,
of class, and craft fraternities," they can be said to have curtailed the
growth of tyranny. But despotism avidly seeks to dissolve those communal ties and to replace them with feelings of narrow self-regard: It
"immures [the people] each in his private life and, taking advantage of
the tendency they already have to keep apart, it estranges them still

more. Their feelings toward each other were already growing cold; despotism freezes them" (xiii). The only antidote to thaw people's hearts and minds is freedom. It alone "can deliver the members of a community from that isolation which is the lot of the individual left to his own devices" (xiv). Here was the old lesson of the *Democracy*, offered once more to a France that had seen a new kind of despotism surface under Napoléon le petit.

The Old Regime, Tocqueville says, tries to achieve three distinct goals. The first is to answer the question, Why France? The tremors that foretold the Revolution were felt in all Europe, but only in France did the earthquake occur. The second object is to indicate how the Revolution issued from the society it so ardently tried to destroy. The third is to explain why the monarchy, once challenged, disintegrated so completely and so suddenly.

The book's three parts also conform to the general structure of *Democracy in America*. Part 1 of *The Old Regime* is really an introductory essay comprising just 20 pages. Part 2, however, concerns the institutions and customs of old France—as volume 1 of the *Democracy* pertains to those of the United States. Part 3 examines the ideas and feelings of prerevolutionary French society, just as the 1840 *Democracy* did for Jacksonian America. The same concerns with customs, mores, laws, institutions, ideas, and feelings recur in this new inquiry.

To understand the French Revolution, Tocqueville contends, one must recognize its fundamentally religious character. Here was a judgment startling in its novelty, since so many of the eighteenth-century philosophers spent so much of their energy furiously attacking the Church. Yet those assaults are misleading, for "it was far less as a religious faith than as a political institution that Christianity provoked these violent attacks" (6). Indeed, "the notion that democratic régimes are necessarily hostile to religion is based on a total misconception of the facts; . . . on the contrary . . . it would seem that a democratic climate is highly favorable to Christianity" (7). And a close examination of the evidence shows how religious the entire Revolution was. It sought to change people's minds and hearts utterly. It established propaganda ministries. Its doctrine was a universal gospel about the rights of man. In short, it was one, holy, catholic, and apostolic. These qualities, in turn, meant that the object of the Revolution itself was the complete overthrow of what had gone before. The tragic irony of the French Revolution was that the ensuing rule was in many ways simply a replica of the fading days of the Old Regime.

But this continuity does not mean that the French Revolution achieved nothing, meant nothing. On the contrary, it accomplished one seemingly immense task—the destruction of feudalism. Yet feudal institutions existed throughout Europe, and throughout Europe were dying in the eighteenth century. This was the case "even in Germany" (16), which Tocqueville had briefly visited to investigate those institutions firsthand. Only in France, however, do we find feudalism overmastered. Why there? "Why did the storm that was gathering over the whole of Europe break in France and not elsewhere?"

It happened there, Tocqueville argues, because of a fundamental contradiction between the high social standing of the nobility, on the one hand, and, on the other, the lack of political and administrative functions they had to perform. In a word, the nobility's privileges remained untouched even as their responsibilities diminished. In the end, they served a purely ornamental purpose, and "at last their mere existence seemed a meaningless anachronism" (30).

So the revolution that destroyed feudalism occurred not in the lands where feudalism was most prevalent, but where it was already virtually extinct.

In making such an argument, Tocqueville subtly alters the terms of the study from one of social structure and politics to one of culture and perception. Everyone had agreed that the Old Regime had been a citadel of feudalism, while the Revolution was the legion that captured and subjugated that fortress. Tocqueville shows that such a perception was incorrect because, in fact, France had already emerged from feudalism. Furthermore, the chief agent of that emergence had been the monarchy itself. The legal instrument wielded by monarchical power to this end was Roman law, "a slave-law" highly serviceable to centralizing monarchs who readily found interpreters to "furnish them at need with legal warrant for violating the law." Indeed, "monarchs who have trampled the laws have almost always found a lawyer ready to prove the lawfulness of their acts," Tocqueville notes (223 n. 1), thinking undoubtedly of the nineteenth as much as the seventeenth century.

The confusion about the Old Regime, then, stemmed from deceptive appearances. Just because the aristocracy was utterly useless did not mean that it was without privilege. And like any threatened group it devoted its waning energies to the protection of those unearned dispensations. But as the century advanced, the gap between privilege and function widened. The Revolution smashed the hollow shell.

By 1750, all administrative functions had been seized from the nobility. Eighteenth-century parish records show that the local lord was "merely one of the inhabitants of the parish, differentiated from the others by certain exemptions and privileges" (27). They did, of course, possess their ancient "feudal rights," but "exactly the same feudal rights were in force in every European land and . . . in most other countries of the continent they pressed far more heavily on the population than in France" (29).

What filled the administrative gap left by the nobility's departure were the *intendants*, agents of the central power whose authority in all matters except in the administration of justice (an important exception, as Tocqueville will emphasize in the drafts for the second volume) was almost absolute. Here Tocqueville presses his theme of appearance and reality one step further. Just as the nobility, who enjoyed special privileges, appeared strong but possessed no real authority, so the intendants exercised great control but had little in the way of social standing: "All-powerful though he was, the Intendant cut a relatively humble figure beside the least representatives of the feudal aristocracy, which had lost nothing of its ancient glamour, and this explains why, though he made his authority felt at every turn, he attracted so little notice" (36). Thus, the centralization of both governmental and administrative power had attained an unprecedented fullness and maturity in France, with the state "playing the part of an indefatigable mentor and keeping the nation in quasi-paternal tutelage" (41). No reader of the *Democracy* can miss the import of these words. In volume 1 of the earlier work, Tocqueville had taken pains to point out the despotic consequences of administrative centralization. His research for *The Old Regime* showed how this tutelary state had actually come into being.

In New England, Tocqueville believed he had found the only examples of free townships in the civilized world. "Among all the nations of continental Europe, one may say that there is not one that understand[s] communal liberty," he had written in 1835 (*DIA*, 62). But his later examination of the French local records caused him to alter this judgment: "I discovered some of the features which had struck me so much in the rural townships of North America: features which I then had—wrongly—thought peculiar to the New World. . . . Transported overseas from feudal Europe and free to develop in total independence, the rural parish of the Middle Ages became the township of New England" (48). The French local liberties, however, had degenerated to mere hollow forms, drained of substantive content by the encroachments of the central power. By the end of the eighteenth century, "as nowadays, there was in France no township, borough, village, or hamlet, however small, no hospital, factory, convent, or college which had a right to manage its own affairs as it thought fit" (51).

Likewise, centralizing forces sucked in judicial functions and left public officials unaccountable to the courts. And the resulting system was, Tocqueville insisted, "taken over en bloc and integrated into the constitution of modern France" (60). Thus were a centralized administration and government cooked up by the old system and presented, as it were, on a platter to the revolutionaries.

The entire traditional interpretation of France's revolution, then, was thrown into question by Tocqueville's findings.

In an elegant and influential study, *Tocqueville and The Old Regime*, Richard Herr tried to direct readers' attention away from the theme of centralization. The conventional opinion about *The Old Regime* holds its central argument to be that centralization, rather than being a product of Napoleonic rule, actually originated in the Old Regime. But, Herr contended, because Tocqueville's discussion of this theme occurs only in the first half of part 2, much of the purpose of the book as a whole "remains to be explained." The themes of centralization and aristocratic decadence, he claimed, are like whitecaps on the sea; while the tides are the social and political institutions of France. But at a still deeper level there runs the "ocean current" of the beliefs, ideas, and feelings of the people, and it is these which constitute the true theme of *The Old Regime*. Herr summarizes Tocqueville's thesis cogently: "By the reign of Louis XVI the transition from aristocratic to democratic society was more advanced in France than in other European countries, while at the same time the public spirit and the institutions necessary for free political democracy had been destroyed by the kings."[8] This interpretation is convincing, although Alan Kahan has added a useful caution in pointing out the importance of class struggle to Tocqueville's analysis.[9] The true object of this work, then, is to display the effect of beliefs and ideas on society and political institutions. In this sense, too, *The Old Regime* is an extension of *Democracy in America*.

The subject of class—"to my mind the historian's proper study," he says (122)—takes up much of the rest of part 2. Tocqueville argues that a double movement was taking place as France approached the Revolution: while on the one hand people were becoming more and more alike, on the other, they were divided into ever smaller, more self-interested groups, each of which was isolated from the rest. The result was a kind of "group individualism" (96) that effectively "brought on most of the diseases to which the old régime succumbed" (97). In an imaginative and strikingly contemporary use of evidence, Tocqueville traces the varying histories of the word *gentleman* in France and elsewhere. In England, "its connotation [is] steadily widened . . . as the classes draw nearer to each other and intermingle. . . . And now in America it is applicable to all male citizens, indiscriminately. Thus its history is the history of democracy itself" (83). In France, by contrast, the term is used "to designate members of a caste" that is still "as exclusive as it was when the term was coined many centuries ago" (84).

So the people were growing ever more similar even as they separated into ever more restrictive groups—"watertight compartments," in fact (100). And because a financial crisis made it imperative that the nation should not coalesce and demand the return of its ancient freedoms, the Old Regime would "spare no pains" (106) to keep the classes apart.

The "group individualism" of French society sprang from two sources. First, the fences between the social classes grew ever higher and more impermeable as the burden of taxation fell more heavily on those least able to bear it—in fact, it was in this very inequality of taxation that the privileges of the aristocracy chiefly consisted. But, secondly, the partitions between classes rigidified because the government, in its centralizing drive, could then "deal only with small, isolated groups of malcontents" (106). The lever of the government's power in accomplishing this end was the bureaucracy. The eighteenth century witnessed a mushrooming of new offices and commissions, all of them involving special privileges for the officeholders. Tocqueville sees the competition for these new appointments as another cause of the people's servility.

The connection between this social compartmentalization and despotism appears again in Tocqueville's notes for the second volume, where he seems to place great emphasis on an assembly at Vizille, which met to express its grievances in 1788. "The main point to be emphasized," he reminded himself, was to be "the momentary union of classes and its immediate result of making the absolute power helpless." The continuity between *The Old Regime* and the second volume is perhaps most striking in these notes on Vizille: "When the French who formed these different classes, breaking through the barriers that had been raised against them, met together in common resistance if only for a single day, it was enough to put the absolute government at their mercy" ("Notes," 178, 180).

Alongside this pernicious compartmentalization, however, freedom endured—albeit freedom of "a peculiar kind . . . of which it is hard for us today to form a clear conception" (108). This freedom consisted of a residue of sturdy customs, immovable, ancient ways of doing things, that persisted in spite of all the pressure for outward conformity produced by the centralizing drive. These customs taken as a whole provided a constant force of resistance; they made the officials balk; they even encouraged a kind of individualism.

Thus does Tocqueville establish the central tension between despotism—discussed in the first chapters of part 2—and liberty. The difficulty emerged from the fact that the freedom under the Old Regime was essentially a negative one—a response to a stimulus, not a way of perceiving and organizing social and political life. Most important, it was not fundamentally *rational*. Instead it was an amalgam of "prejudices, false ideas, and privileges" whose very persistence was the major reason why a "healthy, well-ordered freedom" had failed to emerge (110). Tocqueville had contended in *Democracy in America* that democracy required reason, and indeed that reason was the pivot on which a society would swivel between tyranny or liberty. France's kind of liberty was not the sort to encourage optimism.

The solution should have been to subject the nobility, the owners of such "peculiar freedoms," to the rule of law; instead the nobility was "laid low," and as a consequence "the nation was deprived of a vital part of its substance, and a wound that time will never heal was inflicted on our civilization" (111).

Like the nobility, the clergy, imbued with its archaic traditions of independence from both Rome and Paris, also enjoyed a liberty that has since been destroyed. The material basis of clerical independence was its extensive landownership. When the Revolution deprived the Church of its land, it also severed the clergy from its most important material connection with the laity. It was a huge mistake and only succeeded in "furthering the interests of the Holy See and the temporal power" (112).

Finally, the middle class in the Old Regime also enjoyed robust liberties that have since shriveled. The middle class sought and often won some of the new offices being created in the Old Regime's waning decades, and in so doing enhanced their prestige without compromising their independence (just how Tocqueville does not say). But it was exactly that indispensable autonomy that the Revolution obliterated; now officeholders are completely subject to the central state.

So all three Estates—nobility, clergy, and bourgeoisie (middle class)—enjoyed a kind of rough, irrational, unruly freedom under the Old

Regime that has since vanished; indeed it is here that we can locate the origins of Napoleon III's reimposition of despotic government. After nobility, clergy, and bourgeoisie, there remain to be considered the vast majority of the French people in the eighteenth century: the peasants. In chapter 12, at the end of part 2, Tocqueville analyzes their condition with sympathy and insight. Their situation was worsening in the eighteenth century, as they bore the burdens of taxation and found themselves being progressively cut off from contact with the other classes. The resulting alienation was frightful: a "spiritual estrangement" so "pernicious" (121) and a social and economic isolation so severe that the peasant had no one to rely on but himself. "He was, in fact, cold-shouldered on all sides and treated like a being of a peculiar species" (124). Isolated, poor, and burdened, the peasant became the ruling class's "other." The less actual contact the nobility and middle classes had with him, the more he was stereotyped. Peasants began to be depicted as improvident wastrels who, like freed blacks, were thought to respond only to the incentive of hunger. "It . . . was thought that without the necessity of earning his daily bread, the peasant would not do a stroke of work; that pauperism was the only cure for idleness. I have heard just the same ideas put forward as regards the Negroes in our colonies" (128). Few people in mid-nineteenth century France could write such a sentence with such authority. Tocqueville recognized that what had befallen France's peasantry was analogous to the plight of ex-slaves in the wake of emancipation and of paupers in the new industrial world.

The peasants' response to such isolation was of course to intensify it. As a defense mechanism, "the peasant's upbringing and way of living gave him an outlook on the world at large peculiar to himself, incomprehensible to others." The classes, no matter what the degree of their physical proximity, became "sealed books to each other" (135).

As a consequence of these ever-worsening class divisions that existed in a regime of increasing central control, the nation's cohesion decayed. The more tightly the center closed its grip, it seems, the less the nation as such truly existed. The monarchs got what they wanted: control. But the only technique they would consider to maintain it was a policy of division that eventually rendered the nation itself an illusory construct: "Though the nation came to seem a homogeneous whole, its parts no longer held together. Nothing had been left that could obstruct the central government, but, by the same token, nothing could shore it up" (137).

This devastating social portrait of prerevolutionary France is almost Sophoclean in its force and implications. It is as though we do not have

to see the Revolution unfold to know what will happen—but with fascinated horror cannot divert our gaze.

Thus ends part 2, the description of society and politics. Part 3 begins
a move toward abstraction, toward the history of ideas. Midway through
the eighteenth century, Tocqueville says, a strange kind of fever seemed
to grip France's intellectuals. The malady was one familiar to readers of
the *Democracy*'s second volume: it was the tendency toward the general
and abstract, the infatuation with the simple and mathematical in place
of the messy realities of actual human affairs. What was wanted, these
intellectuals believed, "was to replace the complex of traditional customs
governing the social order of the day by simple, elementary rules deriving from the exercise of the human reason and natural law" (139). "Out
of touch with practical politics," he says, with "little acquaintance with
the realities of public life" (140), their speculations became ever bolder
and at the same time more ethereal. The result was an insoluble contradiction: "Alongside the traditional and confused, not to say chaotic,
social system of the day there was gradually built up in men's minds an
imaginary ideal society in which all was simple, uniform, coherent, equi-
table, and rational" (146).

Here, then, in outline, was the situation in France toward the close of
the eighteenth century. The realm of society and politics was riven with
contradictions, as each group on the social scale suffered incursions on its
chaotic, irrational liberties. These limitations came as a result of the
monarchy's centralizing tendencies, which in turn were driven by a hor-
rendous fiscal crisis. In the domain of ideas, meanwhile, contradictions
also abounded, as the speculative and theoretical tendencies always
latent in French thought were intensified by the rationalistic and mathe-
matizing forces of the Enlightenment. Yet the warring forces within the
social and intellectual spheres were only one aspect of the much broader
problem, since those spheres were also in conflict with one another. The
ideal society envisioned by the intellectuals had virtually no connection
with the unruly and isolated groups that barely constituted a nation
within the borders of France.

What gave way was freedom. The reformers' schemes won out over
the imperfect liberties society enjoyed. Of course, the idea of liberty was
essential to the course of the Revolution; it was just that such freedom
could not be brought down out of the realm of ideas. "Of all the ideas
which led up to the Revolution," Tocqueville wrote, "the concept and
desire of political liberty . . . were the last to emerge, as they were also
the first to pass away" (157).

In his notes for the uncompleted second volume on the Revolution, Tocqueville begins where *The Old Regime* left off, with this passion for the abstract: "The idea of the greatness of man in general, the omnipotence of his reason, and the unlimited extent of his understanding had penetrated and absorbed everyone's thought. . . . In times when passions take over in human affairs, we should attend less to what experienced people think than to what occupies the imagination of dreamers" ("Notes," 153, 155). Something in this infatuation with abstraction immunized even France's greatest lumières against a true understanding of freedom. Voltaire lived in England for three years and came away entranced not with its liberty but with its skepticism. The Physiocrats thought up every prescription for economic growth except free institutions. In fact, these economic theorists were the architects of precisely the "democratic despotism" that Tocqueville had so movingly described at the end of *Democracy in America* 16 years before.

In Tocqueville's opinion, the precipitating event for the Revolution was the decision, in 1787, to overhaul the nation's administrative system. "Though this is hardly mentioned by present-day historians," Tocqueville maintains, "the abrupt, wholesale remodeling of the entire administration which preceded the political revolution had already caused one of the greatest upheavals that have ever taken place in the life of a great nation. This first revolution had an incommensurable influence on the second" (201). Thus, there were two revolutions, as Alan Kahan has maintained. This "first revolution" was not the "political" one of 1789 but was rather "administrative" and social in character.[10] In part 2, Tocqueville would write:

> We often find authors writing before the end of 1788 using such expressions as "things happened in such-and-such a way before the Revolution." We are surprised, since we are in the habit of hearing about the Revolution of 1789. But if we consider the significant actions and public innovations of this year 1788, we see that for centuries there had been no such great change in class relationships or in the government of the country. It was indeed a very great revolution, but one that would soon be lost in the immensity of the one that followed, and so would disappear from the view of history. ("Notes," 179)

It was this first revolution that nurtured the spark of liberty. But it was destined to be suffocated in the second revolution, the one that began in 1789 and ended with the Terror that had claimed Tocqueville's grandfather.

Tocqueville's interpretation of the French Revolution has been enor-
mously influential and has gradually replaced the reigning Marxist view
over the last ten years. "Tocquevillian perspectives are now at the center
of discourse on the French Revolution," writes Seymour Drescher, who
also shows the continuities between Tocqueville's rather cursory treatment of revolution in *Democracy in America* and in the *Recollections*—as
well as the relevance of "Tocquevillian perspectives" to the 1989 revolutions in Eastern Europe.[11]

In his *Recollections*, Tocqueville shows how the Revolution of 1848 was
really a continuation of that of 1789. Thus, we have in Tocqueville's
writings analyses of the so-called first revolution just before 1789 and of
the most recent (hardly the last) one of 1848, but not of 1789 itself.

The *Recollections* of the Revolution of 1848 and its aftermath are
unlike anything else on the Tocqueville shelf of books. By turns intense-
ly personal, caustically humorous, analytical, and tragic, the volume is
not the one to turn to for a narrative of what happened in 1848. While
it contains some superb descriptive passages, its greatest value lies in
what it reveals about the reactions of democracy's leading contemporary
analyst to those stirring, foolish, and tragic events.

In a remarkable recent study, Lawrence Shiner has interpreted the
Recollections as, in part, a series of "tableaux"—both in the sense of a published list or table and of a theatrical scene. *Grandeur* or greatness of spirit, Shiner shows, is put forward by Tocqueville as the criterion of moral
judgment over the historical actors he will present; its antithesis is
petitesse. And, he continues, "When one adds the use of aphorism to the
exemplary function of the portrait and the *tableau*, it becomes clear that
the *Recollections* belongs in the general tradition of the French *moralistes*."
Indeed, he sees the *Recollections* as a work that conceals an underlying
"thematic code" embracing such binary oppositions as liberty/equality,
reform/revolution, disinterest/ambition, and, most important, great-
ness/greed.[12] Shiner's book is one-half of an indispensable tool kit for
those who would fully appreciate the *Recollections*; the other half would
be a history of 1848. With such a literary-critical and historical guide,
the assiduous reader can perceive how the book's hidden structures,
omissions, and distortions can contribute to an understanding of its
many meanings.

Like all Tocqueville's major works, the book is divided into parts; but
in this case, the parts are (or are made to seem!) less of an imposed structure than reflections of the changing conditions under which they were
written. Part 1 was composed at Tocqueville in the summer of 1850. It

contains his impressions of the early "symptoms" of the Revolution and of its outbreak. When Tocqueville's health failed in the autumn of that year, however, his physician insisted on his removal from Normandy, and he and Madame Tocqueville journeyed to Sorrento. Part 2 was written there, in the winter of 1850–51. It brings the story down to the tragic bloodletting of the June Days. Finally, he wrote part 3 in Versailles the following autumn; it concerns his five months as foreign minister.

The book fairly pulses with astringent and sometimes hilarious comments about some of the leading figures in the events of that period. Fair or unfair, they have a fine, emperor's-new-clothes flavor. Of Alphonse de Lamartine, the Republic's first president: "I do not think I ever met in the world of ambitious egoists in which I lived any mind so untroubled by thought of the public good as his" (*R*, 135). Michel Goudchaux, a commissioner for Paris, "was unable to discuss difficulties in the Budget without bursting into tears; yet he was one of the most valiant little men one could meet" (185). One especially famous portrait is that of the Catholic Liberal Lacordaire with his "long, bony neck sticking out of his white cowl [he was a Dominican priest], his shaven head with just a ring of black hair, his narrow face, aquiline nose and fixed, glittering eyes": a vulture (146–47). (Upon Tocqueville's death, Lacordaire would be called upon to occupy his chair in the Académie Française.)

One of the most engaging vignettes, in its own very different way as intriguing as the image of Cavour sitting down with Tocqueville, Beaumont, and Nassau Senior, is the dinner party at which Tocqueville was seated next to George Sand. The occasion was awkward on a number of counts: politically, because Madame Sand favored the revolutionaries; socially, because the poet Prosper Mérimée, who had just ended a fervent but brief affair with Sand, was present as well. (Tocqueville retails the currently fashionable joke about the affair: "They had followed Aristotle's rules in the conduct of their romance, with the whole action obedient to the unities of time and place" [167].) Tocqueville was irritated at first ("I detest women who write"), but over the course of the evening found himself completely "charmed." "All her intelligence seemed to have retreated into her eyes, abandoning the rest of her face to raw matter," he recalled. And with the usual hint of ambivalence that accompanies these portraits, he noted, "She really did have a genuine simplicity of manner and language, which was perhaps mingled with a certain affectation of simplicity in her clothes" (167).

The memoir's scenes of February to June naturally center around Tocqueville's Parliamentary duties. When the Republic was proclaimed, he returned to Normandy for the general election. He describes how he took his alphabetical place in line with all the other electors from his village for the march to nearby Saint-Pierre, where the polling would take place. "When we got to the top of the hill overlooking Tocqueville, there was a momentary halt; I realized that I was required to speak," he recalls. "I climbed to the other side of a ditch. . . . I reminded these good people of the seriousness and importance of the act they were going to perform; I advised them not to let themselves be accosted or diverted . . . but rather to march as a united body with each man in his place and to stay that way until they had voted" (120). Tocqueville won more than 110,000 of the 120,000 votes cast that day.

Returning to Paris, he participated in the Constituent Assembly, which he describes with wit and insight, as he does the invasion of 15 May and the ensuing June Days.

For all the brilliance of composition, however, the analysis of events in the *Recollections* is one that readers of Tocqueville's other works, or even of this exposition of Tocqueville, can foresee. "What struck him and remained for him the essential character of the Revolution of 1848 was the fact that it was directed against society and not the government, the fall of the July monarchy being merely one more contingent event," André Jardin writes.[13] It was this warning—of a revolution against the social structure rather than the government—that Tocqueville had issued in his celebrated speech of 27 January.

That such a revolution would occur, given the dislocations of French society, was something that Tocqueville had, in effect, prophesied since 1835. Democracy in France would have to travel along another path from that which it had followed in America. But, in the very long run, as Tocqueville knew, that might turn out to be just as well. What would finally matter most, he wrote to his friend Corcelle toward the end of his life, was the character of the people, for "political societies are not what their laws make them but what they are prepared in advance to be by the feelings, the beliefs, the ideas, the habits of heart and mind of the men who compose them."[14]

Notes and References

Chapter One

1. Tocqueville to Madame Swetchine, 26 February 1857, in *Oeuvres complètes*, 15 vols., ed. J. P. Mayer (Paris: Gallimard, 1951–), vol. 15, pt. 2, p. 315. Hereafter cited as *OC*, followed by volume, part, and page numbers.

2. Alexis de Tocqueville, *Democracy in America*, trans. George Lawrence, ed. J. P. Mayer (New York: Harper and Row, 1969), 16. Hereafter cited as *DIA*.

3. Alexis de Tocqueville, *Journey to America*, ed. J. P. Mayer, rev. and augmented ed. in collaboration with A. P. Kerr, trans. George Lawrence (Garden City, N.Y.: Doubleday Anchor, 1971), 154–55. Hereafter cited as *J*.

4. *OC*, 15:2:315.

5. André Jardin, *Tocqueville: A Biography*, trans. Lydia Davis with Robert Hemenway (New York: Farrar Straus Giroux, 1988), 70. My indebtedness to Jardin is greater than the testimony provided by citations in endnotes, especially in this chapter.

6. The fragments are published in *OC*, 5:1:37–54.

7. Quoted in Jardin, *Tocqueville*, 89.

8. Tocqueville to Beaumont, 1828 or 1829, *OC*, 8:1:75.

9. Tocqueville to Beaumont, 4 March 1859, *OC*, 8:3:616.

10. François Furet, *In the Workshop of History* (Chicago: University of Chicago Press, 1984), 68–69.

11. Quoted in Jardin, *Tocqueville*, 93. Jardin argues that the recipient was Eugene Stoffels. The J. P. Mayer edition of the *Oeuvres complètes* (13:1:373–75) names Kergorlay.

12. See especially: Burleigh Taylor Wilkins, *The Problem of Burke's Political Philosophy* (Oxford: Clarendon, 1967); Joseph Papin III, *The Metaphysics of Edmund Burke* (forthcoming); Isaac Kramnick, *The Rage of Edmund Burke: Portrait of an Ambivalent Conservative* (New York: Basic Books, 1977); Bruce James Smith, *Politics and Remembrance: Republican Themes in Machiavelli, Burke, and Tocqueville* (Princeton, N.J.: Princeton University Press, 1985).

13. The discussion in Irena Grudzinska Gross's *The Scar of Revolution: Custine, Tocqueville, and the Romantic Imagination* (Berkeley: University of California Press, 1991), 102–45, recognizes the presence of the sublime in Tocqueville, but surprisingly never mentions Burke, who was surely more important to Tocqueville's sensibility than the one aesthetician she does mention, Friedrich Schiller.

14. Edmund Burke, *The Works of Edmund Burke*, 12 vols. (Boston: Little, Brown, 1865–67), 1:110. Hereafter cited as *W*.

15. Wilkins, *Problem*, 149.

16. Smith, *Politics and Remembrance*, 140.

17. They are reprinted in *J*, 343–403.

18. The story, which Tocqueville had read as a boy, perhaps in Metz, was a French translation of Sophie von La Roche's romantic novel *Erscheinungen am See Oneida*. For an interesting account of the background of this novel see Victor Lange, "Visitors to Lake Oneida," *Symposium* 2 (May 1948): 48–74.

19. Chateaubriand, *Atala* and *René*, trans. Irving Putter (Berkeley: University of California Press, 1952). On the shared romantic element, see Eva Doran, "Two Men and a Forest: Chateaubriand, Tocqueville and the American Wilderness," *Essays in French Literature* 13 (November 1976): 44–61.

20. George Wilson Pierson, *Tocqueville and Beaumont in America* (New York: Oxford University Press, 1938), 201–5.

21. Alexis de Tocqueville, *The Old Regime and the French Revolution*, trans. Stuart Gilbert (New York: Doubleday Anchor, 1955), esp. 2, 21.

22. Tocqueville to Louis de Kergorlay, 10 November 1836, *OC*, 8:1:418.

23. Tocqueville to Charles Stoffels, 22 October 1831, in Alexis de Tocqueville, *Selected Letters on Politics and Society*, ed. Roger Boesche, trans. James Toupin and Roger Boesche (Berkeley: University of California Press, 1985), 63.

24. Gustave de Beaumont, "Memoir," in *Memoir, Letters and Remains of Alexis de Tocqueville*, ed. Beaumont (Boston: Ticknor and Fields, 1862), 1:19–20.

25. Quoted in Jardin, *Tocqueville*, 187.

26. John Stuart Mill to Tocqueville [September 1835], *OC*, 6:1:299.

27. Seymour Drescher, *Tocqueville and England* (Cambridge, Mass.: Harvard University Press, 1964), 55–124.

28. Alexis de Tocqueville, *Alexis de Tocqueville's Journey in Ireland, July–August, 1835*, ed. and trans. Emmett Larkin (Washington, D.C.: Catholic University of America Press, 1990), 26.

29. Alexis de Tocqueville, "Report on the Abolition of Slavery," in *Tocqueville and Beaumont on Social Reform*, ed. and trans. Seymour Drescher (New York: Harper Torchbooks, 1968), 98–136. Hereafter cited as "Report."

30. Tzvetan Todorov, *On Human Diversity: Nationalism, Racism, and Exoticism in French Thought*, trans. Catherine Porter (Cambridge, Mass.: Harvard University Press, 1993), 202.

31. Quoted in Jardin, *Tocqueville*, 318. The first passage is from an unpublished letter to Lamoricière; the second, from an essay of October 1841 published in *OC*, 3:1:214.

32. Roger Boesche, "Tocqueville and *Le Commerce*: A Newspaper Expressing His Unusual Liberalism," *Journal of the History of Ideas* 44 (April-June 1983): 277–92.

33. See Mary Lawlor, *Alexis de Tocqueville in the Chamber of Deputies* (Washington, D.C.: Catholic University of America Press, 1959).

34. The speech is reprinted as Appendix III to *DIA*, 749–58; quote on 752–53.

35. Georges Duveau, *1848: The Making of a Revolution*, trans. Anne Carter (Cambridge, Mass.: Harvard University Press, 1984), 120; Blanqui quote, 119–20.

36. Quoted in Jardin, *Tocqueville*, 372.

37. Alexis de Tocqueville, *Recollections*, trans. George Lawrence, ed. J. P. Mayer and A. P. Kerr (Garden City, N.Y.: Doubleday Anchor, 1971), 3–4. Hereafter cited as *R*. Of course, Tocqueville's words are not to be taken completely without irony: see L. E. Shiner, *The Secret Mirror: Literary Form and History in Tocqueville's "Recollections"* (Ithaca, N.Y.: Cornell University Press, 1988), 17–18.

38. R. R. Palmer, "Introduction," *The Two Tocquevilles, Father and Son: Hervé and Alexis de Tocqueville on the Coming of the French Revolution*, ed. and trans. R. R. Palmer (Princeton, N.J.: Princeton University Press, 1987), 148.

39. Tocqueville to Mrs. Grote, quoted in Jardin, *Tocqueville*, 522.

40. Max Weber, "Politics as a Vocation," in *From Max Weber: Essays in Sociology*, ed. and trans. H. H. Gerth and C. Wright Mills (New York: Oxford University Press, 1946), 139.

41. Weber, "Religious Rejections of the World and Their Directions," in *From Max Weber*, 351.

42. Weber, "Science as a Vocation," in *From Max Weber*, 147.

43. David Ingram, *Critical Theory and Philosophy* (New York: Paragon House, 1990), 56–57.

44. Anthony J. Cascardi, *The Subject of Modernity* (New York: Cambridge University Press, 1992), 2, 3.

45. Seymour Drescher, *Dilemmas of Democracy: Tocqueville and Modernization* (Pittsburgh: University of Pittsburgh Press, 1968), 6.

46. Tocqueville to Henry Reeve, 22 March 1837, *Selected Letters*, 115–16.

47. Jürgen Habermas, "Modernity—An Incomplete Project," in *The Anti-Aesthetic: Essays in Postmodern Culture*, ed. Hal Foster (San Francisco: Bay Press, 1983), 4.

Chapter Two

1. Jürgen Habermas, *The Philosophical Discourse of Modernity: Twelve Lectures*, trans. Lawrence Friedman (Cambridge, Mass.: MIT Press, 1987), 16.

2. William Dray, *Perspectives on History* (London: Routledge and Kegan Paul, 1980), 101.

3. *DIA*, 12. Hereafter cited in text in this chapter. For clarity of presentation, one- or two-sentence paragraphs in some passages are presented together without the indentation.

4. Hugh Brogan, *Tocqueville* (London: Fontana, 1973), 28.

5. On Guizot's impact on Tocqueville, see Edward T. Gargan, "The Formation of Tocqueville's Historical Thought," *Review of Politics* 24 (January 1962): 51–52. The text giving the closest approximation to Tocqueville's "Author's Introduction" survey is François Guizot, *History of Civilization in Europe*, trans. William Hazlitt (New York: A. L. Burt, n.d.), esp. 61–72.

6. This last is the argument, more ingenious than fully convincing, of Marvin Zetterbaum in *Tocqueville and the Problem of Democracy* (Stanford, Calif.: Stanford University Press, 1967), 1–19.

7. Bernard Lonergan, *Method in Theology* (New York: Herder and Herder, 1970), chap. 8.

8. In his sprawling, indispensable classic, *Tocqueville and Beaumont in America*, George Wilson Pierson devotes a chapter to "The Design of the *Démocratie*" (739–55), which is, however, chiefly a disquisition on Tocqueville's style, objectives, and doctrines.

9. Jean-Claude Lamberti, *Tocqueville and the Two Democracies*, trans. Arthur Goldhammer (Cambridge, Mass.: Harvard University Press, 1989), 50.

10. On this point, see Jack Lively, *The Social and Political Thought of Alexis de Tocqueville* (Oxford: Clarendon, 1962), 49–50, and, more generally, Robert Nisbet, "Tocqueville's Ideal Types," in *Reconsidering Tocqueville's "Democracy in America*," ed. Abraham S. Eisenstadt (New Brunswick, N.J.: Rutgers University Press, 1988), 171–91.

11. James T. Schleifer, *The Making of Tocqueville's "Democracy in America"* (Chapel Hill: University of North Carolina Press, 1980), 134.

12. Quoted in Schleifer, *Making*, 270.

13. On the position of juge auditeur and Tocqueville's brief but honorable career, see especially Jardin, *Tocqueville*, 73–78; 185–87.

14. See Alan S. Kahan, *Aristocratic Liberalism: The Social and Political Thought of Jacob Burckhardt, John Stuart Mill, and Alexis de Tocqueville* (New York: Oxford University Press, 1992), esp. "Introduction" and chap. 6.

15. Lamberti, *Tocqueville*, 4.

16. Henry Steele Commager, "Tocqueville's Mistake," *Harper's* 269 (August 1984): 72.

17. Cushing Strout, "Tocqueville's Duality: Describing America and Thinking of Europe," *American Quarterly* 21 (Spring 1969): 87–99.

18. For a somewhat different reading of this dichotomy, see Sheldon S. Wolin, "Archaism and Modernity," *Tocqueville Review* 7 (1985–86): 77–88.

19. Leo Marx, *The Machine in the Garden: Technology and the Pastoral Ideal in America* (New York: Oxford University Press, 1964).

20. Robert N. Bellah et al., *Habits of the Heart: Individualism and Commitment in American Life* (New York: Harper and Row, 1985), vii.

21. Perry Miller, "From the Covenant to the Revival," in *The Shaping of American Religion*, ed. James Ward Smith and A. Leland Jamison (Princeton, N.J.: Princeton University Press, 1961), 365.

Chapter Three

1. Lamberti, *Tocqueville*, 163.
2. Emile Durkheim, *The Rules of Sociological Method*, 8th ed., ed. George E. G. Catlin, trans. Sarah A. Solovay and John H. Mueller (1895; Chicago: University of Chicago Press: 1938), 1–13.
3. See especially Edward Pessen, "The Egalitarian Myth and the American Social Reality: Wealth, Mobility, and Equality in the 'Era of the Common Man,'" *American Historical Review* 76 (October 1971): 989–1034; Pessen, *Jacksonian America: Society, Personality, and Politics*, rev. ed. (Homewood, Ill.: Dorsey, 1978), 4–32; Pessen, *Riches, Class, and Power before the Civil War* (Lexington, Mass.: D. C. Heath, 1973), 130–50; Sean Wilentz, "Many Democracies: On Tocqueville and Jacksonian America," in *Reconsidering*, 207–28.
4. *Encyclopedia Britannica*, 9th ed. (New York: Henry G. Allen & Co., 1888), 23:431. The article was reprinted in the next two editions.
5. Seymour Drescher, "Tocqueville's Two *Démocraties*," *Journal of the History of Ideas* 25 (April-June 1964): 201–16.
6. Harold Laski, "Alexis de Tocqueville," in *The Social and Political Ideas of Some Representative Thinkers of the Victorian Age*, ed. F. J. C. Hearnshaw (New York: Barnes and Noble, 1930), 102–9.
7. Theodore Zeldin, *France, 1848–1945*, vol. 2, *Intellect, Taste, and Anxiety* (Oxford: Clarendon, 1977), 983.
8. Lamberti, *Tocqueville*, 135.
9. Koenraad W. Swart, "'Individualism' in the Mid-Nineteenth Century (1826–1860)," *Journal of the History of Ideas* 23 (January-March 1962): 79, 85.
10. Quoted in Schliefer, *Making*, 251.
11. Giving Tocqueville's discussion this label is anachronistic because, as applied to industrial labor, *alienation* is a Marxian concept, and Marx would not compose his notes on it until four years later: Karl Marx, "Alienated Labour," in *Selected Writings*, ed. David McLellan (New York: Oxford, 1977), 77–87. However, because of the conformity of Tocqueville's description to Marx's conception, the use of the term seems proper.
12. A germane example is Daniel Walker Howe, *The Political Culture of the American Whigs* (Chicago: University of Chicago Press, 1979).
13. U.S. Bureau of the Census, *Historical Statistics of the United States, Colonial Times to 1957* (Washington, D.C.: Government Printing Office, 1960), 57.
14. Ralph Lerner, *The Thinking Revolutionary: Principle and Practice in the Early Republic* (Ithaca, N.Y.: Cornell University Press, 1987), 178.
15. G. W. F. Hegel, *Phenomenology of Spirit*, trans. A. V. Miller (New York: Oxford University Press, 1977), 111–19.
16. Hegel, *Phenomenology*, 116.

17. Zetterbaum, *Tocqueville*, 35, 36.

18. Quoted in Schliefer, *Making*, 229.

19. Ann Douglas, *The Feminization of American Culture* (New York: Knopf, 1977), 48–52.

20. Catharine Beecher, *A Treatise on Domestic Economy, for the Use of Young Ladies at Home, at School*, rev. ed. (New York: Harper & Bros., 1846), chap. 1. According to Beecher's biographer, her reading of Tocqueville prompted many of the ideas that appear in this remarkable book, which Massachusetts adopted for use in the public schools. Kathryn Kish Sklar, *Catharine Beecher: A Study in American Domesticity* (New Haven, Conn.: Yale University Press, 1973), 155, 305 n. 1.

21. Lamberti, *Tocqueville*, 221, 222.

22. After extensively casting about for an appropriate phrase, Tocqueville finally and with apparent dissatisfaction used the expression "democratic despotism" in a letter to his brother, 10 July 1838—nearly seven years after he had left the United States. See Lamberti, *Tocqueville*, 313 nn. 69, 74. A cogent recent appraisal of democratic despotism appears in Roger Boesche, *The Strange Liberalism of Alexis de Tocqueville* (Ithaca, N.Y.: Cornell University Press, 1987), chap. 12, esp. 238–46.

Chapter Four

1. Tocqueville, "On the Emancipation of Slaves," in *Tocqueville and Beaumont on Social Reform*, 137–73; quote on 166. Hereafter cited as "Emancipation."

2. Tocqueville to the Countess de Tocqueville, December 25, 1831, *Selected Letters*, 73.

3. Ronald L. Meek, *Social Science and the Ignoble Savage* (Cambridge: Cambridge University Press, 1976); Stuart Woolf, "French Civilization and Ethnicity in the Napoleonic Empire," *Past and Present*, 124 (August 1989): 104.

4. Friedrich Engels, *Origins of the Family, Private Property and the State* (New York: International Publishers, 1942), 5.

5. Lewis Henry Morgan, *Ancient Society* (1877; rpt. Cambridge, Mass.: Harvard University Press, 1964), 16ff.

6. Thomas Jefferson to William Ludlow, 6 September 1824, in *The Portable Thomas Jefferson*, ed. Merrill D. Peterson (New York: Viking, 1975), 583.

7. Arthur O. Lovejoy and George Boas, *Primitivism and Related Ideas in Antiquity* (Baltimore, Md.: Johns Hopkins University Press, 1935), 14.

8. Morgan, *Ancient Society*, 426, 447, 291, 165.

9. G. T. F. Raynal, *Histoire philosophique et politique des établissements et du commerce des Européens dans le deux Indes* (1781), quoted in Woolf, "French Civilization and Ethnicity," 104 n. 18.

10. Lerner, *Thinking Revolutionary*, 176.
11. Alfred Cobban, *A History of Modern France*, vol. 2, *From the First Empire to the Second Empire, 1799–1871*, 2d ed. (Harmondsworth: Penguin, 1965), 106.
12. Tocqueville to Beaumont, 30 August 1829, *OC*, 8:1:80.
13. Edward T. Gargan, *Alexis de Tocqueville: The Critical Years, 1849–1851* (Washington, D.C.: Catholic University of America Press, 1955), 5–7.
14. Guizot, *History*, 61–65, 72–73.
15. See Matthew Mancini, "Political Economy and Cultural Theory in Tocqueville's Abolitionism," *Slavery and Abolition* 10 (September 1989): esp. 152–57.
16. For the tradition of Africans as barbarians, see Philip D. Curtin, *The Image of Africa: British Ideas and Action* (Madison: University of Wisconsin Press, 1964), 63–64.
17. Eric Foner, *Nothing but Freedom: Emancipation and Its Legacy* (Baton Rouge: Louisiana State University Press, 1983), 8–38; Thomas C. Holt, "'An Empire over the Mind': Emancipation, Race, and Ideology in the British West Indies and the American South," in *Region, Race, and Reconstruction: Essays in Honor of C. Vann Woodward*, ed. J. Morgan Kousser and James M. McPherson (New York: Oxford University Press, 1982), 283–313.
18. G. de Beaumont and A. de Toqueville [*sic*], *On the Penitentiary System in the United States and Its Application in France*, trans. Francis Lieber (Philadelphia: Carey, Lea & Blanchard, 1833), 161 note cc.
19. Alexis de Tocqueville, "Memoir on Pauperism," in *Tocqueville and Beaumont on Social Reform*, 1–2. Subsequent references appear in the text. For background and exposition, see Jardin, *Tocqueville*, 242–46; Drescher, *Tocqueville and England*, 134–40; Drescher, *Dilemmas* , 104–12.
20. *Correspondence and Conversations of Alexis de Tocqueville with Nassau William Senior, from 1834 to 1859*, ed. M. C. M. Simpson, 2 vols. in one, 2d ed. (1872; rpt. New York: Augustus M. Kelley, 1968), 1:2.
21. Alexis de Tocqueville, *Journeys to England and Ireland*, ed. J. P. Mayer, trans. George Lawrence and K. P. Mayer (New Haven, Conn.: Yale University Press, 1958), 205 n. 2.
22. Nassau Senior to Lord Althorp, March 1833, quoted in Marian Bowley, *Nassau Senior and Classical Economics* (1937; rpt. New York: Octagon, 1967), 290.
23. A. J. Whyte, *The Early Life and Letters of Cavour, 1819–1848* (1925; rpt. Westport, Conn.: Greenwood, 1976), 101.
24. Cavour, diary of 24 May 1835, in Whyte, *Early Life and Letters of Cavour*, 122.
25. Tocqueville, *Journeys to England and Ireland*, 45, 72.
26. Steven Marcus, *Engels, Manchester, and the Working Class* (New York: Random House, 1974), 65.

27. Tocqueville, *Journeys to England and Ireland*, 105, 108, 107.

28. Marcus, *Engels, Manchester, and the Working Class*, 66.

29. Gertrude Himmelfarb has provided a useful discussion of Tocqueville's attitude to poverty in *The Idea of Poverty: England in the Early Industrial Age* (New York: Knopf, 1983), 147–52.

30. See chap. 1, n. 11.

31. Gustave de Beaumont and Alexis de Tocqueville, *On the Penitentiary System in the United States and Its Application in France* (Carbondale: Southern Illinois University Press, 1964), 34. Subsequent references will be to this edition and appear in the text.

32. Roger Boesche, "The Prison: Tocqueville's Model for Despotism," *Western Political Quarterly* 33 (December 1980): 550–63.

33. Beaumont and Tocqueville, *Penitentiary System* (1833 ed.), 135–36.

34. Arthur Schlesinger, Jr., "Individualism and Apathy in Tocqueville's *Democracy*," *Reconsidering*, 94–109; *DIA*, 506–8.

35. Tocqueville to Louis de Kergorlay, 10 November 1836, *OC*, 13:1:344.

36. Charles de Secondat, baron de Montesquieu, *The Spirit of the Laws*, ed. and trans. Anne M. Cohler, Basia Carolyn Miller, and Harold Samuel Stone (Cambridge: Cambridge University Press, 1989), 59.

37. Boesche, *Strange Liberalism*, 238–41; Boesche, "The Prison," 550–63.

38. Quoted in Schliefer, *Making*, 229.

39. Lynn Marshall and Seymour Drescher, "American Historians and Tocqueville's *Democracy*," *Journal of American History* 60 (December 1968): 526.

Chapter Five

1. Tocqueville to John Stuart Mill, 14 November 1839, *OC*, 6:326.

2. The famous section on blacks appears in *DIA*, 340–63.

3. Seymour Drescher, "Tocqueville and Beaumont: A Rationale for Collective Study," in *Tocqueville and Beaumont on Social Reform*, 210–11 n. 12; Gustave de Beaumont, *Marie, Or Slavery in the United States*, trans. Barbara Chapman (Stanford, Calif.: Stanford University Press, 1959); Alvis L. Tinnin, "Introduction" to *Marie*, xvi.

4. Beaumont, *Marie*, 162.

5. Drescher, "Tocqueville's Two *Démocraties*," 206.

6. *DIA*, 351 n. 41; Beaumont, *Marie*, 158 n.

7. David Brion Davis, *The Problem of Slavery in Western Culture* (Ithaca, N.Y.: Cornell University Press, 1966), 286, 10.

8. William A. Green, *British Slave Emancipation: The Sugar Colonies and the Great Experiment* (New York: Oxford University Press, 1976), 132.

9. Drescher, *Dilemmas*, 158–71; Serge Daget, "A Model of the French Abolitionist Movement and Its Variations," in *Anti-Slavery, Religion, and Reform:*

Essays in Memory of Roger Anstey, ed. Christine Bolt and Seymour Drescher (Hamden, Conn.: Archon, 1980), 64, 71, *passim*.

10. Quoted in Howard Temperley, "Capitalism, Slavery and Ideology," *Past and Present* 74 (1977): 110.

11. Stanley L. Engerman, "Some Considerations Relating to Property Rights in Man," *Journal of Economic History* 33 (1973): 45–46.

12. Herbert S. Klein, *African Slavery in Latin America and the Caribbean* (New York: Oxford University Press, 1986), 258–59.

13. Drescher, *Dilemmas*, 188; Holt, "Empire," 288.

14. James L. Roark, *Masters Without Slaves: Southern Planters in the Civil War and Reconstruction* (New York: Norton, 1977), 108.

15. Quoted in Holt, "Empire," 289–90.

16. Davis, *Slavery in Western Culture*, 433.

17. Robert Nisbet, "Tocqueville's Ideal Types," in *Reconsidering*, 181; David Knight, *The Age of Science: The Scientific World-view in the Nineteenth Century* (Oxford and New York: Basil Blackwell, 1986), 1–10.

18. Stephen Jay Gould, *The Mismeasure of Man* (New York: Norton, 1981), 324–25.

19. Durkheim, *Rules of Sociological Method*, 3.

20. Quoted in G. W. Pierson, *Tocqueville in America* (Garden City, N.Y.: Doubleday Anchor, 1959), 210.

21. François Furet, "Intellectual Origins of Tocqueville's Thought," *Tocqueville Review* 7 (1985–86): 126.

22. Michael Hereth, *Alexis de Tocqueville: Threats to Freedom in Democracy*, trans. George Bogardus (Durham, N.C.: Duke University Press, 1986), 145–65.

23. Bruno Bettelheim, *The Informed Heart: Autonomy in a Mass Age* (New York: Free Press, 1960), 151–53; quote on 151.

24. Drescher, "Tocqueville's Two *Démocraties*," 214–16.

25. Tocqueville to Arthur de Gobineau, 22 October 1843, *"The European Revolution" and Correspondence with Gobineau*, ed. and trans. John Lukacs (1959; rpt. Westport, Conn.: Greenwood, 1974), 212. Subsequent references appear in the text.

26. Alexis de Tocqueville, *On Democracy, Revolution, and Society: Selected Writings*, ed. John Stone and Stephen Mennell (Chicago: University of Chicago Press, 1980), 347.

27. Melvin Richter, "Tocqueville on Algeria," *Review of Politics* 25 (1963): 367.

28. Hereth, *Alexis de Tocqueville*, 158.

29. Ibid., 160–61; quote on 160.

30. *OC*, 3:1:151.

31. John Lukacs, "Introduction," *"European Revolution,"* 14.

32. Tocqueville, "Reflections on English History," a letter probably to Beaumont of 5 October 1828, in *Journeys to England and Ireland*, 28.

Chapter Six

1. Alan Kahan, "Tocqueville's Two Revolutions," *Journal of the History of Ideas* 56 (October 1985): 592.
2. *London and Westminster Review* (January-April 1836): 137–69.
3. Tocqueville to Baron de Bunsen, quoted in Richard Herr, *Tocqueville and the Old Regime* (Princeton, N.J.: Princeton University Press, 1962), 22.
4. Quoted in Herr, *Tocqueville*, 28.
5. François Furet, *Interpreting the French Revolution*, trans. Elborg Forster (New York: Cambridge University Press, 1981), 133.
6. Tocqueville, *The Old Regime*, x. Hereafter cited in text.
7. Alexis de Tocqueville, "Chapters and Notes for His Unfinished Book on the French Revolution (mostly 1857)," in *The Two Tocquevilles*, 147–223. Hereafter cited as "Notes" in text.
8. Herr, *Tocqueville*, 33, 35, 63.
9. Kahan, *Aristocratic Liberalism*, 35–39; 172 n. 100.
10. Kahan, "Tocqueville's Two Revolutions," 587.
11. Seymour Drescher, "'Why Great Revolutions Will Become Rare': Tocqueville's Most Neglected Prognosis," *Journal of Modern History* 64 (September 1992):429–54; quote on 430.
12. Shiner, *Secret Mirror*, 21–33; quote on 33; chart of "thematic code," 90.
13. Jardin, *Tocqueville*, 456.
14. Tocqueville to Francisque de Corcelle, 17 September 1853, *OC*, 15:2:81.

Selected Bibliography

PRIMARY WORKS

Oeuvres complètes d'Alexis de Tocqueville. Edited by Gustave de Beaumont. 9 vols. Paris: Michel Lévy Frères, 1860–66.

Oeuvres complètes. Edited by J. P. Mayer. 15 vols. to date. Paris: Gallimard, 1951–.

ENGLISH TRANSLATIONS

Alexis de Tocqueville's Journey in Ireland, July-August, 1835. Edited and translated by Emmett Larkin. Washington, D.C.: Catholic University of America Press, 1990.

Correspondence and Conversations of Alexis de Tocqueville with Nassau William Senior, from 1834 to 1859. Edited by M. C. M. Simpson. 2d ed., 2 vols. in one. New York: Augustus M. Kelley, 1978. Reprint of 1872 edition.

Democracy in America. Edited by J. P. Mayer, translated by George Lawrence. New York: Harper and Row, 1969.

"The European Revolution" and Correspondence with Gobineau. Edited and translated by John Lukacs. Westport, Conn.: Greenwood Press, 1974.

Journey to America. Edited by J. P. Mayer, translated by George Lawrence. Rev. ed. in collaboration with A. P. Kerr. Garden City, N.Y.: Doubleday Anchor, 1971.

Journeys to England and Ireland. Edited by J. P. Mayer, translated by George Lawrence and K. P. Mayer. New Haven, Conn.: Yale University Press, 1958.

Memoir, Letters and Remains of Alexis de Tocqueville. Edited by Gustave de Beaumont. 2 vols. Boston: Ticknor and Fields, 1862.

The Old Regime and the French Revolution. Translated by Stuart Gilbert. New York: Doubleday Anchor, 1955.

On the Penitentiary System in the United States and Its Application in France. Carbondale: Southern Illinois University Press, 1964.

Recollections. Edited by J. P. Mayer and A. P. Kerr, translated by George Lawrence. Garden City, N.Y.: Doubleday Anchor, 1971.

Selected Letters on Politics and Society. Edited by Roger Boesche, translated by James Toupin and Roger Boesche. Berkeley: University of California Press, 1985.

Tocqueville and Beaumont on Social Reform. Edited and translated by Seymour Drescher. New York: Harper Torchbooks, 1968.

The Two Tocquevilles, Father and Son: Hervé and Alexis de Tocqueville on the Coming of the French Revolution. Edited and translated by R. R. Palmer. Princeton, N.J.: Princeton University Press, 1987.

SECONDARY WORKS

Books

Beaumont, Gustave de. *Marie, Or Slavery in the United States.* Translated by Barbara Chapman. Stanford, Calif.: Stanford University Press, 1959. This romantic novel, also a product of the journey to America, is a blistering attack on racism; the evidence strongly suggests that it represents Tocqueville's views on the question as well as its author's.

Boesche, Roger. *The Strange Liberalism of Alexis de Tocqueville.* Ithaca, N.Y.: Cornell University Press, 1987. A stimulating argument placing Tocqueville's work in the context of his generation's concerns and arguing against categorizing his thought (hence the emphasis on the strangeness of his liberalism).

Brogan, Hugh. *Tocqueville.* London: Fontana, 1973. A rebuke to those who would wield Tocqueville as an ideological weapon in the Cold War, Brogan's short work in the Modern Masters series shows how important it is to see him as a man of his own time and speaking to it rather than as a prophet speaking to the twentieth century.

Drescher, Seymour. *Dilemmas of Democracy: Tocqueville and Modernization.* Pittsburgh: University of Pittsburgh Press, 1968. A comprehensive analysis based chiefly on previously neglected works concerning the social problems that accompanied the transition to industrial society.

―――. *Tocqueville and England.* Cambridge, Mass.: Harvard University Press, 1964. Tocqueville called England "intellectually my second country"; Drescher analyzes the importance of England for Tocqueville's understanding of liberty, despotism, industrialization, and aristocracy.

Eisenstadt, Abraham S., ed. *Reconsidering Tocqueville's "Democracy in America."* New Brunswick, N.J.: Rutgers University Press, 1988. Eleven sparkling, critical essays; far superior to the run of conference-generated anthologies.

Furet, François. *In the Workshop of History.* Chicago: University of Chicago Press, 1984. Contains a typically incisive analysis of Tocqueville's "conceptual system" and of eighteenth-century French views of the American.

―――. *Interpreting the French Revolution.* Translated by Elborg Forster. London: Cambridge University Press, 1981. A major difference between Tocqueville's 1836 and 1856 thoughts on the Revolution can be traced to the ebbing of his early optimism about the prospects for liberty.

Gargan, Edward T. *Alexis de Tocqueville: The Critical Years, 1848–1851.* Washington, D.C.: Catholic University of America Press, 1955. A pioneering and richly detailed biographical study of the years described with such artful selectivity in Tocqueville's *Recollections*, this work also contains one of the best comparative analyses of Tocqueville and Marx—a more popular exercise then than now, but at its best still worth doing.

———. *De Tocqueville.* New York: Hillary House, 1965. The theme of this long essay is Tocqueville's sense of the direction and destiny of Western civilization.

Goldstein, Doris S. *Trial of Faith: Religion and Politics in Tocqueville's Thought.* New York: Elsevier, 1975. The authoritative monograph on a key element of Tocqueville's prescription for the success of democratic liberty.

Hearnshaw, F. J. C., ed. *The Social and Political Ideas of Some Representative Thinkers of the Victorian Age.* New York: Barnes and Noble, 1930. Harold Laski's contribution to this collection is notable for its sensitivity to Tocqueville's inner struggles.

Hereth, Michael. *Alexis de Tocqueville: Threats to Freedom in Democracy.* Translated by George Bogardus. Durham, N.C.: Duke University Press, 1986. Especially useful for its discussion of Algeria, this work is also a meditation on the tension between practical politics and political philosophy.

Herr, Richard. *Tocqueville and the Old Regime.* Princeton, N.J.: Princeton University Press, 1962. With Furet and Kahan, the best source of critical commentary. The main subject of The Old Regime, he argues, is not centralization or even, as Beaumont said, the Revolution itself; rather it is the mores of the French people.

Jardin, André. *Tocqueville: A Biography.* Translated by Lydia Davis with Robert Hemenway. New York: Farrar Straus Giroux, 1988. The definitive work representing a half-century of exhaustive scholarship.

Kahan, Alan S. *Aristocratic Liberalism: The Social and Political Thought of Jacob Burkhardt, John Stuart Mill, and Alexis de Tocqueville.* New York: Oxford University Press, 1992. A major work of comparative historical criticism, this book allows us to move toward a more precise meaning of the slippery term "liberal."

Lamberti, Jean-Claude. *Tocqueville and the Two Democracies.* Translated by Arthur Goldhammer. Cambridge, Mass.: Harvard University Press, 1988. The single most exhaustive commentary on *Democracy in America.* The "two democracies" refers both to the two volumes of Tocqueville's work and to the United States and France.

Lively, Jack. *The Social and Political Thought of Alexis de Tocqueville.* Oxford: Clarendon, 1962. Still standard: comprehensive, judicious, and gracefully written.

Pierson, George Wilson. *Tocqueville and Beaumont in America.* New York: Oxford University Press, 1938. This book did more than any other to spark interest in Tocqueville. It is one of the rarest of scholarly achievements: a work of such deep research on a previously obscure subject that over time it becomes a primary source itself. It takes Tocqueville and Beaumont day by day through their American journey.

Richter, Melvin, ed. *Essays in Theory and History: An Approach to the Social Sciences.* Cambridge, Mass.: Harvard University Press, 1970. Richter's essay in this collection lucidly explains how Tocqueville used Montesquieu in composing *Democracy in America.* This is the best single exposition of Montesquieu's influence on Tocqueville.

Schleifer, James T. *The Making of Tocqueville's "Democracy in America."* Chapel Hill: University of North Carolina Press, 1980. What Pierson does for the journey, Schleifer does for the actual process of composition. Based, like Pierson's work, mainly on an exhaustive study of the Yale Tocqueville Manuscripts Collection.

Shiner, L. E. *The Secret Mirror: Literary Form and History in Tocqueville's "Recollections."* Ithaca, N.Y.: Cornell University Press, 1988. A careful, imaginative, and convincing application of contemporary literary theory to the *Recollections.*

Smith, Bruce James. *Politics and Remembrance: Republican Themes in Machiavelli, Burke, and Tocqueville.* Princeton, N.J.: Princeton University Press, 1985. Republics have memories; traditional societies have custom from "time immemorial." Smith examines the interplay of memory and politics in the thought of three foundational figures.

Todorov, Tzvetan. *On Human Diversity: Nationalism, Racism, and Exoticism in French Thought.* Translated by Catherine Porter. Cambridge, Mass.: Harvard University Press, 1993. Links Tocqueville's liberalism and his nationalism, to the detriment of both.

White, Hayden. *Metahistory: The Historical Imagination in Nineteenth-Century Europe.* Baltimore, Md.: Johns Hopkins University Press, 1973. Contains a dense, tightly argued presentation of Tocqueville as a tragic-realist historian.

Zeitlin, Irving M. *Liberty, Equality, and Revolution in Alexis de Tocqueville.* Boston: Little, Brown, 1971. Focusing mainly on texts rather than historical context, Zeitlin furnishes solid expositions, as well as a comparison with Marx.

Zetterbaum, Marvin. *Tocqueville and the Problem of Democracy.* Stanford, Calif.: Stanford University Press, 1967. The "problem" is how to reconcile human freedom with the inevitability of the democratic revolution; the solution is the application of the art of politics. A particularly nuanced and elegant interpretation.

Articles

Boesche, Roger. "The Prison: Tocqueville's Model for Despotism." *Western Political Quarterly* 33 (1980): 550–63. Tocqueville found in the prisons of Philadelphia the conditions that epitomized despotism as he would later analyze it in the *Democracy.*

————. "Tocqueville and *Le Commerce*: A Newspaper Expressing His Unusual Liberalism." *Journal of the History of Ideas* 44 (1983): 277–92. Combines biography with exegesis and helps to explain the nature of Tocqueville's liberalism.

————. "Why Did Tocqueville Fear Abundance? or The Tension between Commerce and Citizenship." *History of European Ideas* 9 (1988): 25–45. Consumption versus social limits to desire—which will prevail in the long run? Tocqueville was not sanguine.

Drescher, Seymour. "Tocqueville's Two *Démocraties*." *Journal of the History of Ideas* 25 (1964): 201–16. An influential discussion of the differing political contexts in which each of the two parts of *Democracy* was written.

Gargan, Edward T. "The Formation of Tocqueville's Historical Thought." *Review of Politics* 24 (1962): 48–61. Guizot and other key influences who shaped Tocqueville's sense of time.

Gershman, Sally. "Alexis de Tocqueville and Slavery." *French Historical Studies* 9 (1976): 467–83. Excellent discussion of the relevant writings, public and private.

Kahan, Alan. "Tocqueville's Two Revolutions." *Journal of the History of Ideas* 46 (1985): 585–96. Liberty and equality: each had its revolution. Helpful in understanding the writings on the French Revolution, especially part 2.

Lukacs, John. "The Last Days of Alexis de Tocqueville." *Catholic Historical Review* 50 (1964): 155–70. Charges Beaumont, an unbeliever, with having been an "unscrupulous editor" as well for having altered and destroyed some of Tocqueville's letters; argues that, contrary to the impression Beaumont wanted to leave, Tocqueville died in the arms of the Church.

Mancini, Matthew. "Political Economy and Cultural Theory in Tocqueville's Abolitionism." *Slavery and Abolition* 10 (1989): 151–71. Places Tocqueville's antislavery writings in a broad Atlantic abolitionist context and argues that Tocqueville both knew his economics and calculatingly chose the discourse of economics to discuss the problem.

Nisbet, Robert O. "Tocqueville, Alexis de." In *International Encyclopedia of the Social Sciences*, 16:90–95. Edited by David L. Sills. New York: Macmillan, 1968. A standard, perhaps old-fashioned, political-science exposition, but one of unusual clarity.

Pappé, H. O. "Mill and Tocqueville." *Journal of the History of Ideas* 25 (1964): 217–34. Useful for its emphasis on the differences between the two.

Richter, Melvin. "Tocqueville on Algeria." *Review of Politics* 25 (1963): 362–98. An indispensable essay; all subsequent scholars have done is append corollaries to Richter's analysis; certainly the place to start for anyone interested in the problem.

Index

The Author

Matthew Mancini is professor and head of the department of history at Southwest Missouri State University. He received his A.B. from Fordham University and his M.A. and Ph.D. from Emory University. He has also taught at Rice University, where he was visiting associate professor of history; and at Mercer University in Atlanta, where he served as chair of the division of social sciences and organized and directed a program of college education for prisoners. The recipient of a Fulbright Lectureship, he spent a year at Hong Kong Baptist College as senior lecturer in American studies. He was also awarded a Faculty Research Fellowship at the Murphy Institute of Political Economy, Tulane University. In addition to his work on Tocqueville, he is the author of scholarly articles on subjects ranging from *Moby-Dick* to convict labor, and the coeditor of *Understanding Maritain* (1988).